Foundation History

THE TWENTIETH CENTURY WORLD

Fiona Reynoldson

Heinemann

Heinemann Educational Publishers
Halley Court, Jordan Hill, Oxford OX2 8EJ
a division of Reed Educational & Professional Publishing Ltd
MELBOURNE AUCKLAND
FLORENCE PRAGUE MADRID ATHENS
SINGAPORE TOKYO SAO PAULO
CHICAGO PORTSMOUTH (NH) MEXICO
IBADAN GABORONE JOHANNESBURG
KAMPALA NAIROBI

First published 1993

This edition published 1995

97 98 10 9 8 7 6 5 4 3

**British Library Cataloguing in Publication Data is available
from the British Library on request.**

ISBN 0- 435-31688 5

Designed by Ron Kamen, Green Door Design Ltd, Basingstoke

Illustrated by Phill Burrows, Jeff Edwards, Andrew Greenwood
and Peter Hicks

Printed in Hong Kong and bound in China
Produced by Mandarin Offset
The front cover shows German soldiers marching into Paris and a
young boy in the Warsaw Ghetto.

Acknowledgements

The author and publisher would like to thank the following for
permission to reproduce photographs:
AKG London: 3.7C, 3.7H, 3.7I; Bibliothèque Nationale, Paris:
Cover; Bildarchiv Preussischer Kulturbesitz: 3.7R; Bilderdienst
Suddeutscher Verlag: 4.8D; Bildergenbur Schuster / Dr Müller:
6.1B; Bridgeman Art Library: 3.1C; Bridgeman Art Library /
Imperial War Museum: 2.3E, 2.3H, 2.3L; British Library: 2.4A;
Bundesarchiv, Koblenz: 3.7T, 3.7V; Collins Educational: 5.2A; E.
T. Archives: 4.8A, 4.9Z; Mary Evans Picture Library: 1.1C, 4.9V;
Gunn Brinson: 3.7Q; Robert Harding Picture Library: 6.1F;
Robert Harding Picture Library / Glyn Genin: 6.1A; Robert
Harding Picture Library / David Lomax: 6.1E; Hulton Deutsch
Collection: Cover 2.3C, 2.3N, 3.4E, 4.9C, 4.9U; Robert Hunt
Library: 2.1B; Imperial War Museum: 2.3B, 2.3S, 3.6A, 4.1A,
4.3B, 4.5A, 4.8H, 4.9E, 4.9M, 4.9R; International Ladies
Garment Workers' Union Archives / Labor-Management
Documentation Center, Cornell University: 3.7O; David King
Collection: 5.5C; David Low / Evening Standard / Centre for the
Study of Cartoons and Caricature, University of Kent at
Canterbury / Solo Syndication & Literary Agency Ltd: 3.7L;
National Air and Space Museum, Smithsonion Institution: 4.7D;
Netherlands Photo Archive / Charles Breijer: 4.4C; Popperfoto:
3.4A, 3.7S, 4.9E, 4.9P, 5.1D; Topham Picturepoint: Cover, 3.7G,
4.2A, 5.6D; Weimar Archive: 3.7N, 4.6B

Every effort has been made to contact copyright holders of
material published in this book. Any omissions will be rectified
in subsequent printings if notice is given to the publisher.

Details of written sources

In some sources the wording or sentence structure has been
simplified to ensure that the source is accessible.

L. S. Amery, *My Political Life*, extract quoted in J. Wroughton,
(below): 3.5E
BBC, *The Complete Blackadder Goes Forth*, BBC Videos, 1992:
2.1A
Malcolm Brown, *Tommy Goes to War*, J. M. Dent, 1972: 2.2B,
2.3A, 2.3D, 2.3G, 2.3K, 2.3Q, 2.3Y
S. L. Case, *The Second World War*, Evans Brothers, 1981: 4.6A
Brian Catchpole, *A Map History of the Modern World*,
Heinemann, 1982: 3.2A, 3.3A, 5.3C
N. DeMarco, *The World this Century*, Unwin Hyman, 1987: 5.5B
B. Eliott, *Hitler and Germany*, Longman, 1966: 3.4D
J. Fest, *The Face of the Third Reich*, Pelican, 1984: 3.7J
P. Fisher, *The Great Power Conflict after 1945*, Simon and
Schuster, 1993: 5.6A, 5.6B
P. Fisher and N. Williams, *Past into Present, Book 3*, Collins, 1988:
3.4B
History of the Second World War, Purnell, 1968: 4.7B
Totty Howarth, *Twentieth Century History; The World Since 1900*,
Longman, 1979: 4.8E
Nigel Kelly, *The First World War*, Heinemann, 1989: 2.3T, 2.3W
Nigel Kelly, *The Second World War*, Heinemann, 1989: 3.3B,
4.7C, 4.8B, 4.8C, 4.8G
N. Kelly and M. Whittock, *Era of the Second World War*,
Heinemann, 1993: 3.5A, 4.7C
Stephen Lee, *Nazi Germany*, Heinemann, 1989: 3.4D, 3.7M
Mass Observation, files at Sussex University: 4.9D
Jacques Legrand, *Chronicles of the Twentieth Century*, Longman,
1988: 3.2B
C. K. McDonald, *The Second World War*, Blackwell, 1984: 4.7A,
4.9T
Peter Moss, *Modern World History*, Hart-Davis, 1978: 5.2C
Novosti Press Agency, *Recalling the Past*, Moscow, 1985: 3.3C
Alistair and Anne Pike, *The Home Front: Oral and Contemporary
Accounts*, Tressel, 1985: 4.9N
Fiona Reynoldson, *Evacuees*, Wayland, 1990: 5.3F
Fiona Reynoldson, *Prisoners of War*, Wayland, 1990, 4.3A
Fiona Reynoldson, *Propaganda*, Wayland, 1990: 4.9Y
Fiona Reynoldson, *War beyond Britain*, Heinemann, 1987: 2.2A
J. Roberts (Ed), *History of the Twentieth Century*, Purnell, 1968:
5.4C
S. Saywell, *Women at War*, Costello, 1985: 4.4D
Joe Scott, *The World Since 1914*, Heinemann, 1989: 5.1C, 5.2D
R. Seth, *Operation Barbarossa*, Blond, 1964: 4.2B
K. Shephard, *International Relations 1919–39*, Blackwell, 1987:
3.6E, 3.6F
J. Simpkin, *Contemporary Account of the Second World War*,
Tressell, 1984: 4.4A, 4.4B, 4.8I, 4.9G
L. E. Snellgrove, *The Modern World Since 1870*, Longman, 1981:
3.5F, 5.1C
Norman Stone, *Hitler*, Coronet Books, 1980: 3.7U
The Times Atlas of the Second World War, 1989: 3.2C, 5.3B, 5.4C
Ben Wicks, *No Time to Wave Goodbye*, Bloomsbury, 1988: 4.9Q
J. Wroughton, *Documents on British Political History 1914–1970*,
Macmillan, 1973: 3.5D, 3.6B

CONTENTS

1.1 The Twentieth Century – An Overview

The powerful European countries formed two gangs or alliances at the beginning of the 20th century.

= Triple ENTENTE
= Triple ALLIANCE

'The war to end all wars'. No one wanted another war like this.

The First World War 1914–1918

The two gangs or alliances went to war. After four years of fighting the German side lost. Germany had to pay for the damage the war had caused.

The Russian Revolution 1917

Meantime the Russian workers overthrew their leader, Tsar Nicholas II, in 1917. This meant that the rich people were thrown out. The new government was run for the benefit of the workers. It was called a communist government.

Communism

All the other countries around Russia were worried. Supposing their workers rose up and threw out their leaders? The people who worried most were the rich people. They wanted all communists wiped out in every country.

The League of Nations 1919

The League of Nations was set up in 1919. The League was made up of lots of countries who wanted to stop wars. Unfortunately the League was weak.

Italy and Germany in the 1930s – The rise of dictators

Benito Mussolini led Italy. **Adolf Hitler** led Germany. They both wanted to get rid of communists and they wanted their countries to be the greatest in Europe.

B

SOURCE

Germany was blamed for the war and had to pay for all the damage done.

C

SOURCE

Front cover of an Italian newspaper, showing Hitler and Mussolini at a parade in Berlin, 1937.

The Second World War 1939–1945

Only twenty years after the First World War there was another world war which lasted for six years. This time aeroplanes and bombs meant that many civilians died, as well as soldiers.

Winners and losers of the Second World War.

After the Second World War – European countries less powerful

The two world wars cost Britain a great deal of money. By 1945, Britain and several other countries such as France were not rich and powerful any more. So these countries gradually lost their empires in Africa and Asia.

D SOURCE

"Here you are! Don't lose it again

A British cartoonists's comment on the importance of the Second World War.

E SOURCE

At the stroke of midnight India will awake to freedom. It is fitting that we take the pledge of dedication to the service of India and to the still larger cause of humanity.

Adapted from a speech by the first prime minister of India when India became independent from Britain in 1947.

F

SOURCE

The United Nations from 1945

The United Nations was set up in 1945. It was similar to the League of Nations but it had more power to stop wars. However, it could not stop the Cold War.

The Cold War 1945–1991

As soon as the Second World War was over, the USA and the USSR started a Cold War. They argued and threatened each other but they did not fight. This went on for about 50 years.

Questions

1 This unit gives an overview of all the things that you will read about in this book. Write a heading: **The Twentieth Century – An Overview**. Then underneath list on separate lines all the sub-headings in this unit.

2 Look at Source F. Write down whether the following statement is true or false. 'The cartoonist is saying that all the countries in the United Nations voted the way that the Americans wanted them to vote.'

2.1 The First World War – Why did it start?

Wars start because countries cannot solve their arguments by talking.

The First World War started in 1914. There were five main arguments between the countries of Europe.

1 Empires – Britain, France and Germany

An empire is when one country owns land in another part of the world. Britain and France had large empires. As Germany became more powerful it wanted an empire too. This made Germany a rival of both Britain and France.

2 Navies – Britain and Germany

Britain had a huge navy to protect all the ships sailing to and from countries in the British Empire. When Germany started to build a big navy, Britain was worried. A big German navy was a threat to Britain's navy and to the British Empire.

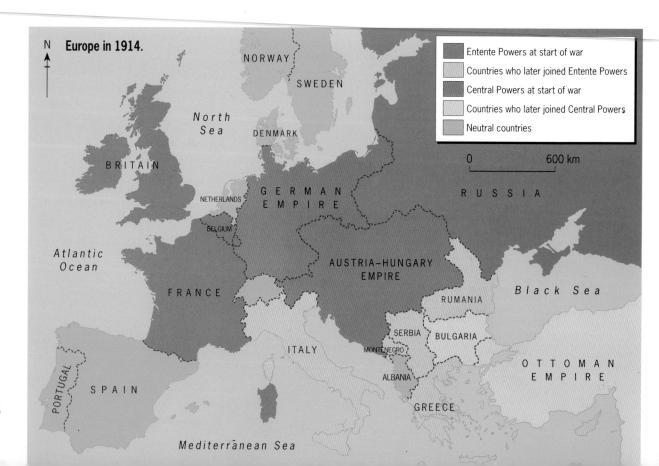

Europe in 1914.

N

	Entente Powers at start of war
	Countries who later joined Entente Powers
	Central Powers at start of war
	Countries who later joined Central Powers
	Neutral countries

0   600 km

NORWAY
SWEDEN
North Sea
DENMARK
BRITAIN
NETHERLANDS
GERMAN EMPIRE
RUSSIA
BELGIUM
Atlantic Ocean
FRANCE
AUSTRIA–HUNGARY EMPIRE
Black Sea
RUMANIA
SERBIA
BULGARIA
MONTENEGRO
ITALY
OTTOMAN EMPIRE
ALBANIA
PORTUGAL
SPAIN
GREECE
Mediterranean Sea

3 Industry – Britain and Germany

By 1914 Germany was producing more coal, iron, steel and cars than Britain.

4 France and Germany as rivals – land

One of the states of Germany had taken some land from France in a war in 1871. France was deeply angry and wanted the land back.

5 Russia and Austria-Hungary as rivals – the Balkans

Russia and Austria-Hungary were bitter rivals. Both countries wanted to control the Balkans (see maps on pages 4 and 8). Russia wanted to control the Balkans by helping the Serbs to unite all Slav people. Austria-Hungary wanted to stop the Serbs uniting Slav peoples.

On 28 June 1914 the Austrian Archduke, Franz Ferdinand, was shot dead by Gavrilo Princip, a Serbian student. This event sparked off the First World War. The diagram (below) shows what happened.

B SOURCE

An Italian cartoon of Kaiser Wilhelm, the leader of Germany.

Questions

1 Write down a heading: **The five arguments between the countries of Europe**. Under the heading, write down the five arguments. (They are numbered 1 to 5. You can make the list by writing down the sub-headings.)

2 Look at the list of arguments you have written in Question 1. Which five European countries were mainly involved in the arguments that led to war?

3 Which event sparked off the First World War?

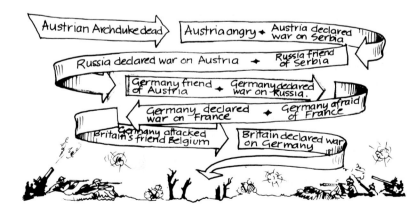

Austrian Archduke dead → Austria angry → Austria declared war on Serbia

Russia declared war on Austria → Russia friend of Serbia

Germany friend of Austria → Germany declared war on Russia.

Germany declared war on France → Germany afraid of France

Germany attacked Britain's friend Belgium → Britain declared war on Germany

How the fighting started.

2.2 The First World War – What happened?

The Schlieffen Plan

The Germans planned to sweep through Belgium and defeat France in a few weeks. Then they could turn and fight Russia.

The attack on Belgium

On 3 August 1914 the German army marched into Belgium. However, Britain had a treaty with Belgium. This treaty said that Britain would protect Belgium so Britain sent the **British Expeditionary Force (BEF)** to help to fight the Germans.

Failure of the Schlieffen Plan

Together the British and French won the **Battle of the Marne** (5–11 September). The Schlieffen Plan had failed. The Germans stopped. Both sides dug trenches to protect themselves. By December 1914 the trenches stretched all the way from the English Channel to Switzerland.

A

SOURCE

The BEF crosses to France, 9–17 August 1914

It was 9 August 1914. The BEF was made up of 90,000 soldiers, 15,000 horses and 315 guns. They were loaded aboard ships for France. Each soldier carried:

5.4 kg clothing
7.6 kg rifle and ammunition
1.2 kg trench tools
3.7 kg webbing
4.4 kg pack
2.5 kg rations, water.

From Fiona Reynoldson 'War beyond Britain', 1987.

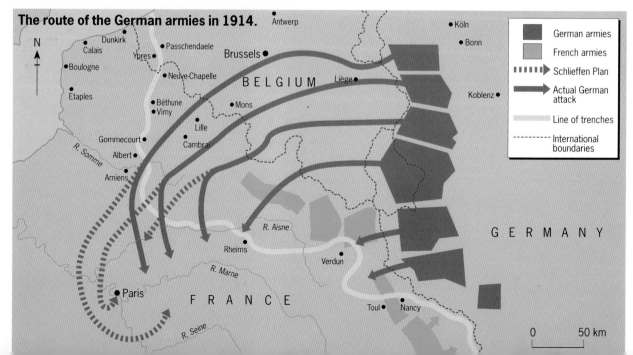

The route of the German armies in 1914.

The Western Front

In the First World War the fighting took place on several fronts. There was the Eastern Front where Russia fought against Germany and Austria. There was fighting in Turkey and there was also fighting at sea and in the air. For the British and French, most of the battles took place on the Western Front.

The Western Front was about 600 kms long.

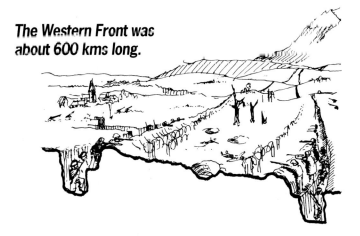

For four years the French and British faced the Germans in deep trenches. Both sides protected their trenches with barbed wire. Both sides had machine guns, mines and artillery. Thousands of soldiers on both sides died trying to attack enemy trenches.

1917

The Russian people overthrew their leaders and stopped fighting the Germans in 1917. This meant Germany could concentrate on fighting the British and French. However, at the same time, the **United States of America (USA)** joined the war on the side of Britain and France.

March 1918

The Germans were desperate to defeat Britain and France before the Americans could send over thousands of fresh soldiers to fight. So the Germans attacked and pushed the British and French back towards Paris. But it was a last effort. The British and French, soon joined by American soldiers, fought back. The Germans retreated. A cease fire or armistice was agreed at 11am on 11 November 1918. The war was over.

Questions

1 Read **The Schlieffen Plan** on page 10. What was the Schlieffen Plan? Write two sentences.

2 Read **1917**. Why was 1917 such an important year in the war?

3 When did the war end?

B

Each man must fight on to the end. The safety of our homes and the freedom of mankind depend upon each one of us.

From General Haig's message to the British troops in April 1918.

2.3 The Western Front: A Study in Depth

This study looks at what it was like to be a soldier on the Western Front. It also looks at the way people left at home in Britain felt about the war.

The war starts – 4 August 1914

Britain declared war on Germany and thousands of people took to the streets cheering. Men of all ages rushed to join the army. They rushed from boring jobs or hard lives or rich homes. They rushed to glory and excitement and a chance to go abroad. Everyone said the war would be over by Christmas. Half a million men had joined the army by September 1914.

'Pals' battalions

The government encouraged friends to join up together. So all the young men from a village or town might join one battalion. (A battalion was about 1000 soldiers). Large cities like Sheffield and Manchester often raised several battalions of local men. The soldiers fought together and died together. Whole 'pals' battalions were almost wiped out on 1st July 1916 at the Battle of the Somme.

Propaganda, pressure and patriotism

The government made posters showing how wicked the Germans were. The posters said the Germans had murdered babies and nuns on their march through Belgium. This propaganda made people feel very patriotic (proud of their country). The British were good. They wanted to fight the bad Germans. Even young men who were not keen to join up felt under pressure. If a young man was not in uniform, people wanted to know why. So through patriotism or pressure, many young men found themselves on the Western Front in France.

A SOURCE

In September 1914 the Northern Foxes Football team of Leeds met together. Someone suggested that the whole club should enlist. It was put to the vote and passed. They joined the Leeds 'pals' battalion.

From M. Brown, 'Tommy Goes to War', 1978.

B SOURCE

Perhaps the most famous of all the recruiting posters, Lord Kitchener's appeal for men. By a clever technique wherever you stand this picture seems to be pointing directly at you.

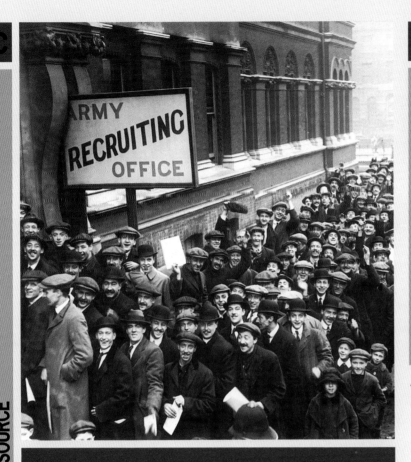

Smiling recruits outside an army recruiting office in London in 1915.

Some boys even lied about their age to get into the army. One boy, Valentine Strudwick joined up at the age of 13 years and 11 months. He was killed one year later by a German shell.

Stalemate 1914

Barbed wire, machine guns, mines and heavy artillery stopped either side moving forward. So the two sides stayed put and dug miles of complicated trenches to shelter in. By December 1914 the war had reached a **stalemate**.

I thought it would be the end of the world if I didn't pass. When I came to have my chest measured, I took a deep breath and puffed out my chest. The doctor said, 'You've just scraped through.' I told my mother and she said I was a fool.

A soldier remembers the day he signed up.

Question

Read **Propaganda, pressure and patriotism**. Match the Heads and Tails.

Heads	Tails
Propaganda	love of your country.
Patriotisim	making you do something.
Pressure	telling you the enemy was doing bad things.

The front line trenches

Look at the diagram showing a cross-section through a **front line** trench. The trenches were dug two metres deep. There were wooden boards called **duckboards** in the bottom of the trench. **Sandbags** protected the top of the trench from enemy bullets but soldiers had to be careful to keep their heads down or they would be shot by enemy snipers. The **machine guns** were stationed along the trench. They could fire 600 bullets a minute.

Support and reserve trenches

When soldiers had finished their four day stint in the front line trenches they made their way to the support trenches where they spent another four days. If there was a German attack the soldiers could rush back to the front line but if all was quiet they went to the reserve trenches for eight days. However, soldiers often stayed for longer in the front line if there was fierce fighting. Usually the reserve trenches were more comfortable. There were better latrines (toilets), kitchens, more dugouts and stores. The whole system of trenches could stretch back as much as eight kilometres from the front line.

The trench system.

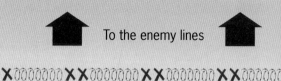

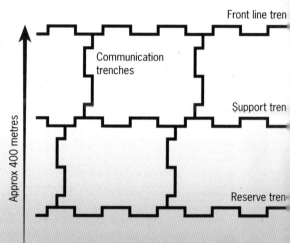

To the enemy lines

No-Man's-Land

Front line tren

Communication trenches

Approx 400 metres

Support tren

Reserve tren

Trenches were dug in zigzags to prevent the enemy firing along the whole trench if they captured a small pa

Cross-section through a front line trench – a soldier spent four days in the front line.

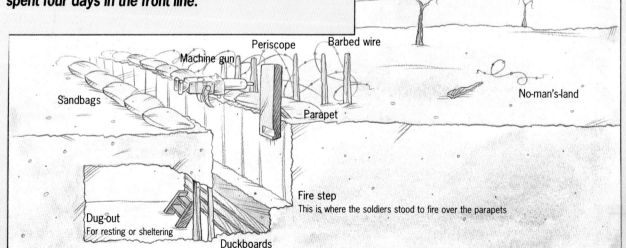

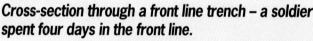

Periscope

Machine gun

Barbed wire

Sandbags

Parapet

No-man's-land

Fire step
This is where the soldiers stood to fire over the parapets

Dug-out
For resting or sheltering

Duckboards

E

Just before dawn a German machine gun lets rip. A Vickers gun replies from our side. Just to let Jerry know we're awake.

From George Coppard, 'With a Machine Gun to Cambrai', 1969.

'Hell', a contemporary painting by the French artist Georges Leroux. It shows a First World War battlefield.

Everyday life – the early morning

The early morning was quiet. In summer the birds would be singing. If **No-Man's-Land** was narrow, the British soldiers could hear the Germans coughing or calling out to each other as they woke up. In winter, the cold, wet and mud made life a misery. The men slept in long johns, wool vests, sheepskin jerkins, home knitted cardigans, layers of newspapers and oiled waistcoats. They covered all this with a greatcoat and still felt cold when they woke up. Summer or winter both sides started the day by firing at each other to show that they were still there and alert.

Questions

1 Look at the diagram called **The trench system**.
   a What are the names of the three parallel lines of trenches?
   b What was No-Man's-Land?
   c Why were the trenches dug in zig-zags?

A day's work – sentry duty, food, trench work and weapons

The soldiers were not fighting all the time, but there were many jobs to do. About one third of the men were on sentry duty. One third spent the morning going back to the support trenches to collect food, water, letters, ammunition, bandages and so on. The other third had to repair the trenches and this could take up a lot of the day. Then all the soldiers had to clean their weapons. A rusty or dirty gun could cost a soldier his life.

Lice, rats and flies

It was difficult to have a good wash so lice were a constant irritation to the soldiers. They made them scratch and this could lead to boils and skin disease. The lice hid in the seams of clothes and it could take hours to pull them out and crush them with a thumbnail.

Other diseases could be spread by the millions of flies all over the battlefields. The flies lived on the tonnes of manure produced by all the horses. But much as the soldiers hated these they hated the rats more. The rats ate any spare food they could find as well as eating the fly infested dead bodies in No-Man's-Land after a battle.

H
SOURCE

An advertising poster issued in 1915.

Health

In the good weather many men in the trenches kept in better health than they had in Britain. Many of the soldiers came from very poor homes. In the army they got better food than they had ever known and they lived out of doors in the sunshine. However, when the winter came it was a different story. The cold and wet caused many diseases such as trenchfoot and pneumonia.

Food

The food was brought up to the front line trenches by soldiers. Most of the food was in tins or jars including the butter, porridge and stew but not the bread. If the carrier fell in a shellhole, the food was mixed up, wet and filthy. If he was killed it might not get there at all. Water came up in big round drums and had to be treated with chloride to kill the germs in it. If the soldier was on a quiet part of the front the food came regularly and was edible. If there was fighting or shelling going on it was a different story.

Fighting on the Western Front

It was during the First World War that machine guns and barbed wire were used for the first time by both sides in a European war.

A sandbag full of rations. A lot of food like butter, porridge and stew was put in jars or tins to keep it dry. If a carrier fell in a shell hole everything got wet, including the letters at the top.

Coughs, colds and trenchfoot were all a result of living in wet clothes and boots.

Questions

1 Read **A day's work**.
  a There were three types of jobs to be done each day. Write a sentence about each one.
  b What did all the soldiers have to do each day?

2 Read the next section. What three animals made life awful for the soldiers?

3 Read **Health**. What sort of diseases did the soldiers get in winter?

4 Trenchfoot was very painful but some soldiers did not take precautions to avoid getting it. Why do you think that was?

Machine guns

The last time Britain had fought a major war was 100 years before. In those days a good soldier could fire four bullets a minute from his musket. In 1914 a machine gun could fire 600 bullets a minute, so one machine gunner could cut down hundreds of advancing soldiers.

Barbed wire

Barbed wire had barbs as thick as fingers. Putting rolls and rolls of barbed wire in front of trenches meant that the enemy could not reach your own trenches.

How to win the war – a policy of attrition

You cannot win a war by sitting in a trench. You have to get up and capture the enemy's land. The Generals in charge of the soldiers tried to think up ways of doing this. One way which they tried over and over again was called a **policy of attrition**. They tried to wear down the enemy. They attacked again and again hoping that the other side would run out of soldiers and guns first. This policy meant that thousands of soldiers were cut down by machine guns as they rushed across No-Man's-Land to attack the enemy trenches.

K

SOURCE

A knife edge pain in the lungs and the coughing up of a greenish froth of the stomach and the lungs, finally resulting in death.

Lance Sergeant Elmer Cotton describes the effects of chlorine gas in 1915.

L

SOURCE

Victims of a gas attack.

How to win the war – gas

At the second battle of Ypres in 1915, the Germans used gas for the first time. It was devastating.

'A strange green mist, a running mass of men in agony, a four-mile gap without a defender.'
(from 'Memoirs' by B. Liddell Hart.)

The gas had done what no attacking soldiers had done. It had broken through the trenches. Soon the British and French were using gas too. However, gas was not going to win the war. Too often the wind changed direction and the gas blew back. Both sides developed gas masks and gas alarms.

How to win the war – artillery

Huge artillery guns were used to fire shells from behind the trenches, across No-Man's-Land and into the enemy trenches. The British used 170 million shells during the war but often only churned the ground in No-Man's-Land to mud and shell holes, making it harder to cross.

Questions

1 Read **Fighting on the Western Front**.
What two things were used for the first time in a European war?

2 Read **Machine guns**. Why was a machine gun more deadly than a musket?

3 What do you think people meant when they said that British soldiers were 'lions led by donkeys'?

M

SOURCE

A First World War tank.

How to win the war – tanks

If you could build a metal box on wheels that bullets would bounce off, you could drive over the German trenches. This was the idea behind **tanks**. Many generals thought the tanks were a waste of time. But some people in the government liked them. They said: 'You aren't winning the war. This new machine might.' In fact it worked very well on the hard, chalky land at the Battle of Cambrai in 1917. However, the tanks often broke down or got bogged down in mud and shell holes. They were not reliable enough in the First World War.

Casualties on the Western Front

Of nearly five million men who joined the British Army during the war, one in five was killed and a further two out of five were wounded.

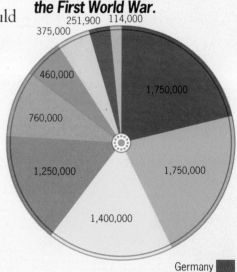

Number of servicemen killed in the First World War.

251,900   114,000
375,000
460,000
1,750,000
760,000
1,250,000   1,750,000
1,400,000

Germany
Russia
France
Austria-Hungary
Great Britain
Italy
Turkey
British Empire
United States

A mass burial of war victims. One in five British soldiers was killed in the war.

Conscription – having to join the forces

In 1914 men had flocked to join the army. But as the war went on they were less keen to volunteer. Therefore in 1916, the government passed the **Military Service Act**. Single men between the ages of 18 and 41 had to join the army, navy or air force. Later married men were conscripted too.

Conscientious objectors

Some men believed that war was wrong. They would not fight. Some were sent to work on farms. Some even helped in the front line rescuing wounded soldiers. But some men would not do anything to help the war at all. Many were sent to prison and 71 died there from ill treatment while in prison.

War in Britain

Meanwhile Britain itself was under attack. **Zeppelin** airships and German bombers carried out air raids. About 1400 people died and this made the British very angry. They turned their anger on Germans living in Britain as well as men who were conscientious objectors.

SOURCE

'James Humphreys has obtained exemption from military service on condition of munition working.'

From the diary of the Rev. A. Clark, 1917.

Questions

1 a Read **How to win the War – tanks**. Write one sentence describing what a tank was.
   b Some British soldiers thought tanks were useless; others thought they were wonderful. When would they be useless and when would they be wonderful?

2 Read **Conscription**. What did the Military Service Act say?

3 Read **Conscientious objectors**. Some soldiers had sympathy for conscientious objectors and some hated them. Can you account for these two views?

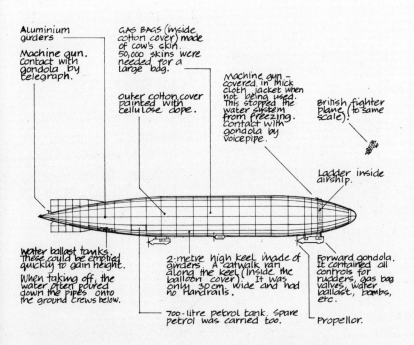

Aluminium girders

Machine gun. Contact with gondola by telegraph.

GAS BAGS (inside cotton cover) made of cow's skin. 50,000 skins were needed for a large bag.

Outer cotton cover painted with cellulose dope.

Machine gun – covered in thick cloth jacket when not being used. This stopped the water system from freezing. Contact with gondola by voicepipe.

British fighter plane (to same scale).

Ladder inside airship.

Water ballast tanks. These could be emptied quickly to gain height. When taking off, the water often poured down the pipes onto the ground crews below.

2-metre high keel made of girders. A catwalk ran along the keel (inside the balloon cover) It was only 30cm wide and had no handrails.

Forward gondola. It contained all controls for rudders, gas bag valves, water ballast, bombs, etc.

700-litre petrol tank. Spare petrol was carried too.

Propellor.

A Zeppelin was about as long as two football pitches.

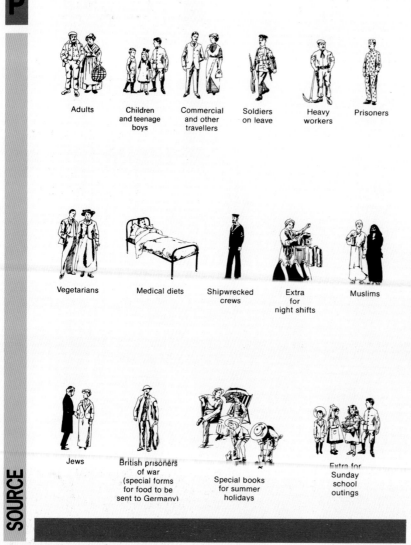

Adults

Children and teenage boys

Commercial and other travellers

Soldiers on leave

Heavy workers

Prisoners

Vegetarians

Medical diets

Shipwrecked crews

Extra for night shifts

Muslims

Jews

British prisoners of war (special forms for food to be sent to Germany)

Special books for summer holidays

Extra for Sunday school outings

Different people had different ration books.

By 1918 we were so fed up we wouldn't even sing 'God save the King'. Never mind the bloody King we used to say; it should have been 'God save us'.

Private J.A. Hooper, 7th Green Howards Regiment.

We all heard we must grow more food so I went to work on a farm setting potatoes.

From Gilbert Stone (ed.), 'Women War Workers', 1917.

Life at home

As the war went on life became more difficult at home. Much of Britain's food came from overseas. The German navy sank as many British ships as it possibly could and by 1917 there was only six weeks supply of food left in Britain. Something had to be done to make sure that food was shared out.

Rationing

The government set up a Ministry of Food which brought in rationing in 1918. Each person was allowed a set amount of meat, tea, butter, sugar, bacon and ham and so on.

Questions

1 Read **Life at Home** and **Rationing**.
   a Where did much of Britain's food come from?
   b What did the German navy do?
   c What did the Ministry of Food do in 1918?

2 Does Source Q prove that the soldiers no longer wanted a king?

Defence of the Realm Act (DORA)

This Act or law was passed at the beginning of the war. It gave the government great power for as long as Britain was at war. The government could take over the railways and industries and it could **censor** newpapers. Furthermore, many people noticed that drunkenness was a huge problem. So the government passed a law that limited the times that pubs opened. It also allowed beer to be watered down.

Women and the war

With so many men fighting, women were needed to work in all sorts of jobs from farming to steel-making, from driving ambulances to sweeping chimneys. By the end of the war many men were impressed with the work women had done. Men were forced to change their views about women being second-class citizens. After the war in 1918 women were given the vote, although they had to be aged 30 or more. Men could vote at 21.

Questions

1 **a** What did DORA stand for?
  b Write down one thing that DORA allowed the government to do.

2 Read **Women and the war**. Why were men forced to change their views about women being second-class citizens?

SOURCE

Women munition workers, painted in 1917, by E.F. Skinner. The artist was appointed by the government to paint pictures of the war.

News from the Front

Food shortages, war work and bombing raids were part of life from 1914 to 1918. But worry about loved ones at the Front dominated life. It was said that by 1918 there was not a family in Britain which had not lost someone – killed or badly wounded. All through the war there was the constant fear of receiving a telegram with the news that a son, brother, husband or father had been killed.

His mother and his sister were standing in the middle of his returned kit which included the tunic torn back and front by the bullet, the khaki vest dark and stiff with blood.

Vera Brittain describes how her fiance's relatives received his kit after he had been killed in France.

I have been asked to send you and your family the utmost sympathy on the death of your husband....He died almost instantaneously, while on duty, as the result of a shell bursting in his trench.

Letter from a platoon sergeant to a soldier's widow.

The Bradford 'pals' battalion suffered heavy casualties in 1916. The local press reported the losses week after week.

LOCAL HEROES OF THE GREAT ADVANCE.

"The Work they did was Absolutely 'Top Hole'"—A C.O.'s Testimony.

The end of the war

By November 1918, the German troops on the Western Front were on the run. At home the German people had reached breaking point and there were riots in the streets. So at 11 am on 11 November 1918 a ceasefire or armistice was agreed. The war was over.

Y

SOURCE

This battle is the best I have ever had. We were on the Germans before they could get their machine guns working and a nice few Germans were killed.

A letter home from a soldier talking about an attack made on 6 November 1918.

W

SOURCE

By 1917 the civilian mood of patriotism and romantic hero worship of the early years gave way to a desire to just see the war through to a victorious conclusion.

Scottish Record Office, 'The First World War', 1986.

X

SOURCE

TO THE
MEN OF CHELMSFORD
WHO FELL IN THE
GREAT WAR

The war memorial in Chelmsford, taken in the 1920s.

Questions

1 Read **News from the Front**.
   a What was part of life for people from 1914 to 1918?
   b What did most people worry about most?
   c How did people usually learn that some member of the family had been killed?

2 Read **The end of the war**. Write down the time and date of the armistice.

3 Use all the sources in the depth study and use the text to discuss the following:
   a How much did the way people thought of the war change between 1914 and 1918?
   b Did everyone think the same?

2.4 The Price of Peace

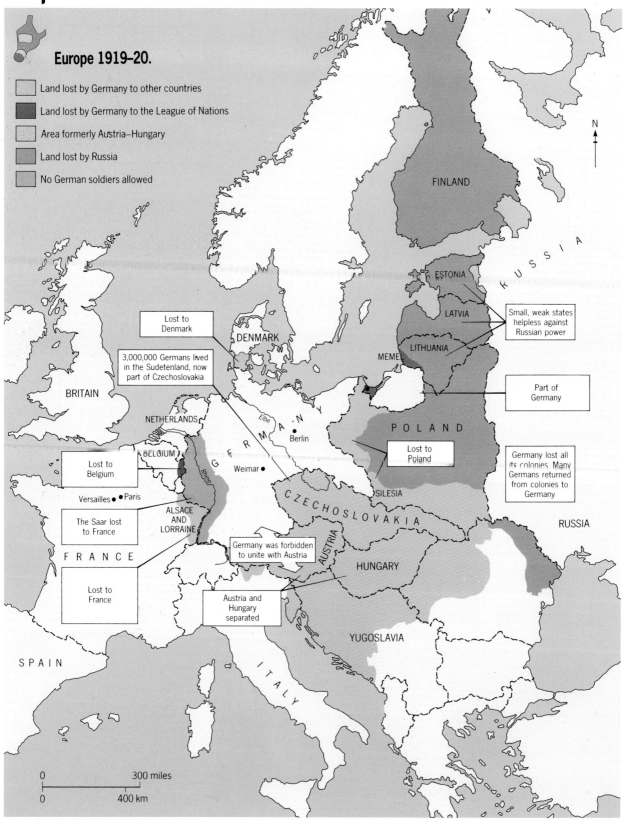

Europe 1919–20.

- Land lost by Germany to other countries
- Land lost by Germany to the League of Nations
- Area formerly Austria–Hungary
- Land lost by Russia
- No German soldiers allowed

N

FINLAND

RUSSIA

ESTONIA

LATVIA

Small, weak states helpless against Russian power

LITHUANIA

MEMEL

Part of Germany

Lost to Denmark

DENMARK

3,000,000 Germans lived in the Sudetenland, now part of Czechoslovakia

BRITAIN

NETHERLANDS

Elbe

POLAND

G E R M A N Y

Berlin

Lost to Poland

Germany lost all its colonies. Many Germans returned from colonies to Germany

BELGIUM

Lost to Belgium

Rhine

Weimar

SILESIA

C Z E C H O S L O V A K I A

RUSSIA

Versailles   Paris

The Saar lost to France

ALSACE AND LORRAINE

Germany was forbidden to unite with Austria

AUSTRIA

HUNGARY

F R A N C E

Lost to France

Austria and Hungary separated

YUGOSLAVIA

SPAIN

I T A L Y

0   300 miles
0   400 km

Making peace

The countries which had won the First World War were called the **Allies**. They did not want another war. They made a peace treaty. The peace treaty said two things. First, there must be no big **empires** in Europe any more. Second, Germany must be punished.

End of the big empires

The big empires of Russia, Germany, Austria-Hungary and Turkey had broken up during the war. The Allies made lots of small countries from the big empires.

The Treaty of Versailles 1919

The Treaty of Versailles was the peace treaty that ended the war. The Germans hated it. The treaty said:
1   The Germans started the war.
2   The Germans had to pay for the bombed houses and factories.
3   The Germans could only have a small army.
4   The Germans could not have any tanks, submarines or warplanes.
5   The Germans had to give up land and colonies.
6   The Germans must never unite with Austria.

The Price of War for France
250,000,000 cubic metres of trenches to fill in
320,000 km of barbed wire to pull up
300,000 houses destroyed
1,000 bridges blown up
6,000 factories gutted

A

SOURCE

PEACE AND FUTURE CANNON FODDER

The Tiger: " Curious! I seem to hear a child weeping !"

A cartoon drawn in 1919. It shows the leaders of the Allies. They have just signed the Treaty of Versailles. Children born in 1919 would be old enough to be soldiers in 1940.

Questions

1 Read the first paragraph. Fill in the gaps.
The countries which won the war were called the _____. The peace treaty said that _____ must be punished.

2 Read **The Treaty of Versailles** and the green box. Which country do you think would want to make Germany agree to No. 2 on the list?

3 Look at Source A and read the caption. Why is the child crying?

3.1 The Russian Revolution 1917–24

1917 was the year of the Russian Revolution. What caused this?

Tsar Nicholas II and the poor

The Tsar had complete power in Russia before the First World War. He used the army and secret police to control the country. He was enormously wealthy and lived in luxury while most Russian people were peasants or factory workers who were very poor.

People against the Tsar

Many educated middle-class people wanted more freedom of speech. The Tsar agreed to set up a parliament in 1905, but although he did this very little changed. This was serious because another group of people wanted far greater changes.

Karl Marx and the Bolsheviks

Marxists liked the ideas of Karl Marx. He was a German writer who said that the workers should rise up and take control of their country. The best known Marxist group was the **Bolsheviks** who were frequently hunted and caught by the Tsar's secret police.

The First World War

In 1914 Russia became entangled in the First World War and it was a disaster. The Russian army was defeated and people lost faith in the Tsar's ability to run the country as well as the war.

Revolution, February 1917

In February 1917 there were riots in the city of Petrograd and the Tsar sent soldiers to quell the riots. However the soldiers refused to fire on the rioters and the Tsar realized he had lost control. The Tsar abdicated (gave up the throne).

The Tsar had complete power in Russia before 1917.

The effects of the First World War on Russia		
	1914	1917
% of men in the army	15	56
Grain produced (million tons)	67	57

Food Prices 1917 (roubles)		
	July	Oct
Cheese (lb)	1.60	5.40
Sausages (lb)	1.00	6.00

The war had a devastating effect on Russia.

C

SOURCE

A painting showing the storming of the Winter Palace, the headquarters of the Provisional Government.

Revolution, October 1917

After the Tsar gave up the throne a Provisional (temporary) Government was set up but it was soon overturned by the Bolsheviks led by Lenin in October 1917. Seeing how hopeless the war was for Russia, Lenin signed the **Treaty of Brest-Litovsk**. This gave vast areas of Russia to Germany but Lenin was not worried. He was buying time to make Russia strong again.

The Civil War in Russia 1918–21

It took a long time for Russia to recover because the anti-Bolsheviks decided to fight. They called themselves the Whites. Lenin's Bolsheviks were called the Reds. The civil war between the Whites and the Reds went on until 1921. The Reds won and in 1923 the Bolsheviks changed their name to the Communist Party. Russia became known as the **Union of Soviet Socialist Republics (USSR)**.

Questions

1 Read **Tsar Nicholas II and the poor** and look at Source A.
  a How did Tsar Nicholas live?
  b How did most people in Russia live?

2 Look at Source B.
  a What per cent of men were in the army in 1914?
  b What percent of men were in the army in 1917?
  c How does Source B help you understand why there were revolutions in Russia in 1917?

3.2 The League of Nations

Woodrow Wilson

Woodrow Wilson was the President of the USA. He wanted all the countries in the world to work for peace. He called this a **League of Nations**. So the League was set up in 1920 and over 50 countries joined it.

What the League of Nations hoped to do

Wilson hoped all the countries would help each other. If one country was attacked all the members of the League would refuse to trade with the attacker. The League also worked to stop other things like slavery and drug trading.

The League's successes – arguments

In 1920 Sweden and Finland argued. They both wanted the same piece of land. The League made them agree rather than fight about it. The League settled several arguments between countries.

A

SOURCE

The League quickly turned into a talking shop, led by the countries which had won the First World War.

From B. Catchpole, 'A Map History of the Modern World', 1982

How the League of Nations worked.

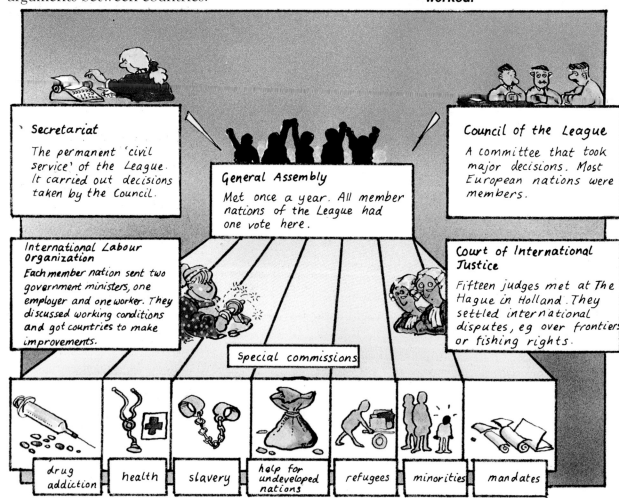

Secretariat

The permanent 'civil service' of the League. It carried out decisions taken by the Council.

General Assembly

Met once a year. All member nations of the League had one vote here.

Council of the League

A committee that took major decisions. Most European nations were members.

International Labour Organization

Each member nation sent two government ministers, one employer and one worker. They discussed working conditions and got countries to make improvements.

Court of International Justice

Fifteen judges met at The Hague in Holland. They settled international disputes, eg over frontiers or fishing rights.

Special commissions

drug addiction | health | slavery | help for undeveloped nations | refugees | minorities | mandates

The League's successes – for working people

The League set up the International Labour Organization. Its first director was a Frenchman. He was called Albert Thomas. He wanted to help all the working people in the world.

The League's successes – slavery

At the end of the war slavery was still legal in many countries. The League worked hard to stop this. They talked to governments. They pointed out how bad slavery was. By the 1930s slavery was illegal in most parts of Africa. It was still legal in some parts of the Middle East.

The League's problems – the USA

After the war Woodrow Wilson stopped being President of the USA. Wilson had worked hard for the League of Nations. But the new President was not interested. He felt everyone in the USA was fed up with Europe. So the USA did not join the League of Nations.

The League's problems – the USSR and Germany

The USSR did not join the League of Nations for several years. Germany left the League in 1933. As the USA had not joined either, this meant that three big countries did not really support the League.

The League's problems – no teeth

The League of Nations was like a big lion with no teeth. It had no way to make people do what it said. For instance, in 1923 Lithuania attacked and took the port of Memel from Germany. The League of Nations said Lithuania must give it back to Germany. Lithuania just said no. The League of Nations had no way to make Lithuania give Memel back. When people saw the League was not working they soon ignored it.

B **Jan 16 1920:** The League of Nations met for the first time today but the Americans were absent.

From 'Chronicle of the Twentieth Century', 1988.

C **March 1933:** Japan leaves the League of Nations. **October 1933:** Germany leaves the League of Nations.

From 'The Times Atlas of the Second World War', 1989.

Questions

1 Read **Woodrow Wilson**.
  a Who was Woodrow Wilson?
  b What did he want?
  c How many countries joined the League of Nations?

2 Look at the picture on page 30.
  a What did the General Assembly do?
  b What did the special commissions do?

3 Read Source B. How does it show that the League was weak?

3.3 Challenges to Peace

The League of Nations

The League of Nations was set up after the First World War. It was hoped the League would be able to stop any further wars.

Japan and China

Japan was a strong country and had a big, well trained army. Japan wanted more land to house its growing population. It also wanted more raw materials like coal, iron, oil and rubber. Japan decided to invade Manchuria in northern China.

1931–7

Japan invaded Manchuria in 1931. China asked the League of Nations for help but, although the League said that Japan was in the wrong, it could not do anything. Japan just left the League of Nations in 1933, and in 1937 invaded the rest of China.

A

SOURCE

The Manchurian affair showed that the League of Nations could not keep world peace.

From B.Catchpole, 'A Map History of the Modern World', 1982.

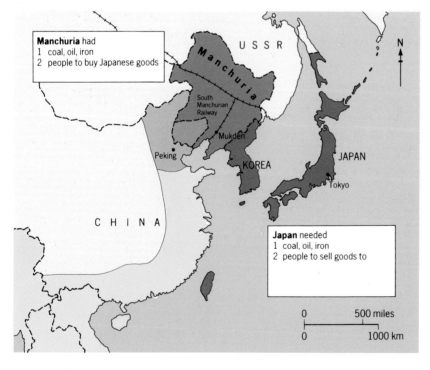

Manchuria had
1 coal, oil, iron
2 people to buy Japanese goods

Japan needed
1 coal, oil, iron
2 people to sell goods to

0   500 miles
0   1000 km

Japanese expansion in Asia in the 1930s.

Japan gets more land
- By 1920s
- 1931–2
- 1933
- 1935–6
- After 1937

Italy

Mussolini was the leader of Italy and he wanted to have a great empire. Mussolini saw how easily Japan had taken land from China. He decided to attack Abyssinia (now known as Ethiopia).

The Abyssinians asked the League of Nations for help. The League said that no one was to sell goods to Italy. However, this did not include steel, copper or oil (just the things needed to fight a modern war) because Britain and France did not want to annoy Italy. They were afraid Italy would be driven to become close friends with Germany.

What happened 1935

Italy defeated the Abyssinians who had very few modern weapons. Then Mussolini left the League of Nations.

Rome-Berlin Axis 1936

Just as Britain and France had feared, Mussolini and Hitler signed an alliance between Italy and Germany.

The Spanish Civil War

In 1936 civil war broke out in Spain. Hitler and Mussolini helped the Spanish Nationalists (led by General Franco) to win the war. The League of Nations did nothing. Everyone realized how weak it was. This was noticed by Adolf Hitler, who realized he could build up Germany's army without the League doing anything.

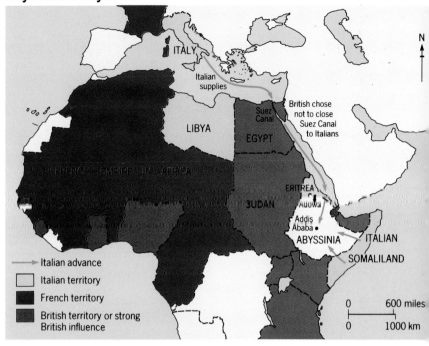

Italy invades Abyssinia.

- → Italian advance
- Italian territory
- French territory
- British territory or strong British influence

ITALY · Italian supplies · Suez Canal · British chose not to close Suez Canal to Italians · LIBYA · EGYPT · FRENCH EMPIRE IN AFRICA · SUDAN · ERITREA · Adowa · Addis Ababa · ABYSSINIA · ITALIAN SOMALILAND · N · 0 600 miles · 0 1000 km

Questions

1 Read page 32.
   a What was it hoped that the League would do?
   b Why did Japan invade Manchuria?
   c What does Source A say was important about the Manchurian affair?

A

Crowds cheer as German soldiers enter the Rhineland, 7 March, 1936.

B

The 48 hours after the march into the Rhineland were the most nerve-racking of my life.

Said by Adolf Hitler to one of his generals.

Adolf Hitler and what he wanted

In 1933 Hitler became the ruler of Germany. He and the **Nazi Party** wanted Germany to be powerful again. So Hitler took Germany out of the League of Nations. Then he ordered Germans to build new tanks, submarines, ships and warplanes. He ordered that every young man had to have army training in the new, bigger German army.

Britain, France and Italy disagree 1935

1935 saw the return of the coal and steel land of the Saar to Germany (taken away after the First World War). The same year Britain allowed Germany to have a bigger navy. This annoyed France. Italy fell out with France and Britain over Abyssinia. So agreement between these three countries was at an end.

The Rhineland 1936

Hitler got more daring. In 1936 he sent German soldiers

C

Germany gets more land.

D

Perhaps you will find me one morning in Vienna.

Said by Hitler to the leader of Austria, in 1938.

into the Rhineland. (This was forbidden after the First World War.)

The German people shouted and cheered. Hitler held his breath. But the League of Nations did nothing.

Hitler and Austria 1938

Hitler wanted to unite Germany and Austria. He told the Austrian leader, **Von Schuschnigg**, that Austria must have Nazi party people in the Austrian government. Von Schuschnigg asked the Austrian people to vote on whether they wanted such a close friendship with Germany. When Hitler heard this he was furious. He ordered the Nazis in Austria to rebel and force Von Schuschnigg to resign. On 12 March 1938, German soldiers marched into Austria and united the two countries.

The League of Nations was in tatters and Britain and France did nothing.

Questions

1 Read **Adolf Hitler and what he wanted**. Make a list of all the things that Hitler did.

2 Look at Source C.
   a Which three countries were most worried when Hitler took the Rhineland?
   (S=Sweden, Cz=Czechoslovakia, F= France, Sw=Switzerland, P=Poland, H=Holland, D=Denmark, B=Belgium)
   b Would any other countries be worried? Which ones?
   c Sources A and E are official German photographs. How might this affect the way historians use them as evidence?

SOURCE

Austrians cheer as German soldiers enter Vienna, 14 March, 1938.

3.5 Peace at Any Price?

Fear of war

In the 1930s many people were afraid of war. They still remembered how bad the First World War had been. So rather than stand up to Hitler, Britain and France let him have his way. This was called **appeasement** (trying to keep the peace).

Czechoslovakia 1938

Czechoslovakia was one of the countries next door to Germany. Part of Czechoslovakia was called the Sudetenland. Many Germans lived there (see map on page 37). Hitler wanted the Sudetenland to become part of Germany. Czechoslovakia wanted to keep it.

What Chamberlain did

The British Prime Minister at the time was called Chamberlain. He tried to sort the problem out. He talked to the Czechoslovakian leader, Benes. Benes said Germany could have the part of the Sudetenland where most of the Germans lived. Chamberlain thought that this seemed fair. He took this offer to Hitler. But Hitler said this was not enough. He wanted all of the Sudetenland.

Hitler got his way

On 28 September Chamberlain and several other leaders met Hitler. They said Hitler could have all of the Sudetenland. (No one had asked the Czech people what they thought.) Hitler was delighted. He said he would not ask for any more land. Everyone wanted to believe him.

A The British Prime Minister, Chamberlain, flew to Germany on 15 September 1938, to try to persuade Hitler not to fight (Czechoslovakia).

From N. Kelly, M. Whittock, 'Era of the Second World War', 1993.

B Chamberlain says Hitler has agreed to stop wanting more land.

C I felt it my duty to strain every nerve to avoid another Great War

Said by Neville Chamberlain in 1938.

D We have been defeated. Czechoslovakia will soon be taken over by the Nazi regime.

Said by Winston Churchill in September 1938.

E Chamberlain had letters of congratulation from the king of the Belgians, and from thousands of ordinary people from all over the world. There would be no war.

From L.S. Amery, 'My Political Life', 1959.

How Czechoslovakia was divided in 1938.

Given to Germany at Munich

Seized by Poland, September

Given to Hungary by Germany and Italy, October

F Chamberlain decided it was fair to give the Sudetenland back to Germany.

From L. Snellgrove, 'The Modern World Since 1970', 1968.

G To go into battle without our Empire behind us is unthinkable.

Said by Henderson, British Ambassador to Berlin, September 1938.

Why did Chamberlain choose appeasement?

Questions

1 Read the first paragraph.
Copy out the right meaning of the word 'appeasement' from the list below.

1 Eating mushy peas
2 Getting angry
3 Giving in to keep peace
4 Pleasing a friend

2 Look at the cartoon opposite.
Make a rough copy with the right number of bubbles.
Fill the empty bubbles with the ones you think are best from the list below.
Fear of war
Sympathy for Germans at Versailles Treaty
Dislike of loud noises
Fear the Empire will not help

3.6 1939: The Collapse of Peace

Hitler goes too far

Hitler thought he could take any land he wanted. He thought that no one would try to stop him. First he took over nearly all of Czechoslovakia in March 1939. Then, a week later, he seized Memel from Lithuania. Meanwhile, Hitler's ally, Italy, invaded Albania. Britain and France were horrified. They felt they could not trust Italy and Germany any more.

The Nazi-Soviet Pact: made between Germany and the USSR

Things got worse. Germany and the USSR signed an agreement (pact). This pact said that they would not be enemies. They would not fight each other. They would share Poland's land between the two of them.

March 1939: Hitler took all of Czechoslovakia. Britain promised to defend Poland.

From J. Wroughton, 'Documents on British Political History', 1973.

Tug-of-war over Danzig.

There is no question of sparing Poland. There will be war. Our job is to isolate Poland.

Said by Hitler to his generals in 1939.

Welcoming the German soldiers.

Final steps to war, 1939.

Legend:
- Germany by the end of 1938
- Seized by Germans, March 1939
- Seized by Hungary, March 1939
- Dominated by Germans
- Invaded by USSR, September 1939
- Invaded by Germans, September 1939

The invasion of Poland

On 1 September 1939, Germany invaded Poland. Britain and France had had enough. They saw that they would have to do something to stop Hitler. They saw that Hitler would not stop taking land unless he was forced to.

War at last

On 3 September 1939, Britain and France finally declared war on Germany.

E

SOURCE

We will fight for Polish freedom. Every Polish house will be a fortress which the enemy will have to take by storm.

From a Polish newspaper, 1939.

F

SOURCE

We secured peace for our country for one and a half years.

Said by the Russian leader, Stalin, to explain the 1939 Pact.

Questions

1 Read **The Nazi-Soviet Pact**. Fill in the gaps.
Germany signed a pact with _____. They would not _____ each other.

2 Look at Source C. What town did Germany and Poland argue over?

3 Look at Source A. Choose the sentence which best describes the picture:
The woman is crying with joy now the soldiers have come.
The woman is sad because the soldiers have come.

4 Read **The invasion of Poland**. What effect did the invasion have?

In 1933 Adolf Hitler became the leader of Germany. He was already the leader of the Nazi Party. Who were the Nazis? What was it like to live under Nazi rule?

Hitler was born in Austria in 1889.

As a young man he earned a poor living painting postcards.

In 1914 the First World War broke out. Hitler joined the German army. He was a brave soldier and won the Iron Cross.

In 1918 Hitler was in hospital when he heard that Germany had lost the war.

Hitler leapt from one shell crater to another. Suddenly he was confronted by French soldiers. . . 'Surrender,' he commanded, 'behind me is a whole company of soldiers.' The Frenchmen threw away their weapons. Single-handed Adolf Hitler took them prisoner.

From an official book about Hitler used in German schools in the 1930s.

The Swastika. This emblem, adopted by the Nazis, dates back to ancient civilizations, where it was used in religious art.

The beginnings of the Nazi Party 1919–23

Hitler could not believe that Germany had lost the First World War. He felt the leaders of Germany had betrayed the German people.

Hitler joined the German Workers' Party and soon came to lead it. He changed the name to National Socialist German Workers' Party (known as the Nazi Party).

The Munich Putsch (Revolt)

Hitler made sure the Nazi Party had its own soldiers. They were called the **SA** or **Stormtroopers** or **Brownshirts**. In 1923 he used these Stormtroopers to try and seize power in the city of Munich in Germany. He failed but was only sent to prison for five years because the judges were sympathetic to him. He only served eight months.

Mein Kampf ('My Struggle')

While he was in prison Hitler wrote his life story and called it *Mein Kampf*. It is not a very good book but it contains Hitler's ideas on how to rule Germany.

Hitler's ideas

a **The supremacy of the Aryan race:** He believed that the people of North Europe were better than any other race.

b **The supremacy of Germany:** Germany was a great power and should have a big army again. Then Germany should be allowed to have land from other less important countries such as the USSR.

c **One strong ruler:** The Nazis did not believe in democracy. They wanted one strong ruler who had power to control everyone.

d **Anti-communism:** The Nazis hated communism. They thought it could not be strong government. They wanted to wipe out communists.

e **Anti-socialism:** Although the Nazi Party had started off being a German Workers' Party, Hitler moved away from these ideas because he wanted money from the big industrial bosses.

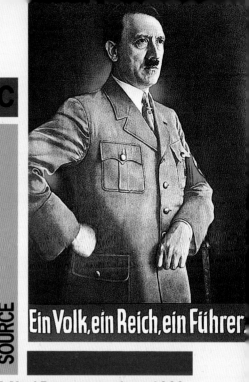

SOURCE C

Ein Volk, ein Reich, ein Führer.

A Nazi Party poster from 1938. The slogan says 'One People, one Empire, one Leader!'

Questions

1 Read **The beginnings of the Nazi Party**.
What was the full name of the Nazi Party?

2 Read **Hitler's ideas**. Write a list of his five ideas.

3 Source A is from a book published by the Nazis. Does this mean that the story it tells isn't true? Explain your answer.

How did the Nazis win power in Germany?

After the war Germany had many problems. There were not enough jobs. Germany had to pay money to the winning countries because Germany was blamed for the war. Prices went up and up. At one time a person could walk into a cafe and order a cup of coffee at one price. By the time she had drunk the coffee the price had gone up. All this made people cross and willing to listen to Hitler's ideas about creating jobs and making Germany rich.

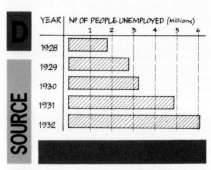

SOURCE D

Unemployment in Germany 1928–32.

The United States of America and the slump 1929

For a time in the 1920s, things in Germany got better and no one listened to Hitler. Then in 1929 a terrible slump took place in the USA. Overnight huge businesses went bankrupt. People lost their jobs. Thousands of people became poor. Because the USA was poor it wanted to get money back from countries it had lent money to. One of these countries was Germany. Having to pay back money to the USA made Germany poor again. People lost their jobs. They lost their savings. This was Hitler's chance.

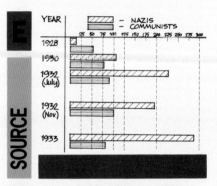

SOURCE E

Seats won by the Nazis and Communists in the Reichstag elections, 1928–33.

Hitler becomes leader of Germany 1933

Hitler was a brilliant speaker. People stood and listened to him for hours at a time. He said he would make Germany great and rich again. So many people voted for Hitler and the Nazi Party. Some other people liked the ideas of the communists so Hitler worked hard to put them down.

The Reichstag elections

The Reichstag was the German Parliament. Both the Nazis and the Communists won more and more seats in the Reichstag until 1933 when Hitler and the Nazis easily beat the Communists (see Source E).

Hitler as Chancellor

After the Reichstag elections of 1933, Hitler had won so many seats that the President, **Hindenburg**, asked Hitler to become the Chancellor of Germany.

SOURCE F

The vote enabling Hitler to rule with complete authority, without asking the Reichstag goes through by 441 votes to 94.

*The Reichstag on fire,
27 February 1933.*

The burning of the Reichstag, 1933

On 27 February 1933, the Reichstag building was burnt down. A Dutch communist confessed to starting the fire. This was a godsend for Hitler. He said that there was a communist plot against the German government and he panicked everyone into allowing him great power. He stopped all freedom of speech and freedom of the press (newspapers).

The Enabling Law

Hitler wanted full power in the Reichstag. So he decided to introduce an **Enabling Law**. This would let him rule with complete power but he had to get the members of the Reichstag to agree to it first. He did three things. First he struck a deal with the Centre Party. Second he threw out all the communist members of the Reichstag. Third he surrounded the Reichstag building with Stormtroopers and members of the SS (his personal soldiers). Most of the members were too frightened to vote against Hitler so the Enabling Law was passed. Hitler now had **absolute power**. Source F shows the Reichstag now meeting in the Opera House, after the fire in February 1933. Goering is watching the members with binoculars to see how they are voting.

Questions

1 Read **How did the Nazis win power in Germany?**
   Write down three of Germany's problems.

2 How could an historian use Source D to explain why Hitler and the Nazis came to power in Germany?

3 Look at Source F and read **The Enabling Law**.
   a Why do you think so many people voted for Hitler's Enabling Law?
   b What do you think might have happened to the 94 who voted against Hitler?

Why did the German people support the Nazis? H

Many German people were discontented after the First World War. They hated the **Treaty of Versailles** which said that Germany was to blame for the war. They hated France for taking the Ruhr (a rich part of Germany) from them just because they could not pay France the war debts they owed. They hated the **inflation** when money and savings became worthless. By the slump of 1929 they had no faith in the government and they hated the lack of jobs.

Children playing with German banknotes in 1923.

SOURCE

'I WILL MAKE GERMANY STRONG & RICH AGAIN!'

'THERE WILL BE JOBS!'

'JEWS AND COMMUNISTS MADE US LOSE THE WAR!'

A Nazi Party poster from 1932. The slogan says, 'Our last hope – Hitler'.

'He's our last chance.' I heard over and over again. After all the Nazis are only a minority in government... and if the worse comes to the worst, the army can turn the Nazis out.

Account from an Englishman living in Germany in the early 1930s.

Hitler's promises

Hitler promised to make Germany rich and powerful again. He promised jobs for all and blamed the Jews and the communists for making Germany lose the First World War.

Hitler – 'Our Last Hope'

Many German people saw Hitler as a last hope. He was a strong leader. But he not only gave them hope he also used his Stormtroopers (SA) and his personal army (SS) to threaten anyone who spoke against him.

Questions

1 Read **Why did the German people support the Nazis?** Write down the things that the Germans hated.

2 Look at the drawing on page 44. Write down the things that Hitler promised.

How did Hitler stay in power 1933–39?

Hitler used **power**, **propaganda** and **popularity** so that he could stay as the leader of Germany.

Power – Hitler as Führer

Hitler used his power to crush anyone or any group that spoke against him. He banned all political parties except the Nazis.

When President Hindenburg died, Hitler made himself both President and Chancellor. He called himself **Führer** and from then on all members of the army swore a personal oath of loyalty, not to Germany, but to 'Adolf Hitler, Führer of the Reich'.

K The Führer has been told that the Jew, Markus Luftgas, was sentenced to two and a half years in prison. The Führer desires that Luftgas should be sentenced to death.

A letter issued by one of Hitler's staff to a provincial governor.

Power – The Night of the Long Knives

Hitler knew that the generals of the ordinary German army did not like the SA. Hitler needed to keep in with the army and was, himself, worried about the growing power of the SA. On 30 June 1934 Hitler ordered the SS to execute Ernst Röhm and other SA leaders. This became known as the Night of the Long Knives. This broke the power of the SA, made Hitler popular with the army and strengthened the SS.

A cartoon from the 'Evening Standard' of 3 July 1934. Hitler is holding the gun, Goering is carrying a spear and Goebbels is on his knees behind Hitler.

Power – the Gestapo

Hitler set up the Gestapo in 1933. These were secret police who hunted out anyone who might be against Hitler. By 1939, there were well over 100,000 people in prison for opposing Hitler and about 20,000 in concentration camps run by the SS.

Power – trade unions

Trade unions were banned and the Nazis controlled workers through their own trade union called the **German Labour Front**.

Power – religion

Hitler tried to remain on good terms with the Protestant and Catholic Churches. But gradually Church support for Hitler became less as it became obvious that the Nazis persecuted the communists, the Jews and anyone else who opposed them.

Hitler wanted to shut down Catholic Youth Movements so that all young people joined the Hitler Youth. In 1937, the Pope spoke out against Nazism. Hitler then sent nuns and priests to labour camps together with several hundred Protestants who spoke out against the Nazis.

A Nazi propaganda poster showing Hitler as the saviour of Germany.

N

SOURCE

Propaganda – newspapers and radio from 1933

Once Hitler controlled all the newspapers, people only knew what he wanted them to know. Hitler put Joseph Goebbels in charge of propaganda. Not only did Goebbels keep an eye on what the newspapers were saying, he also controlled the radio. Throughout the 1930s, more and more homes had radios. All the radio programmes said how wonderful the Nazis were.

Propaganda – posters, music and art

Goebbels had lots of posters made showing Hitler as a wonderful leader. He also had many posters made putting down anyone who opposed Hitler. Other posters were made showing that other races such as the Jews and black people were inferior to the Germans. In the Nazi propaganda, the Jews were not only inferior but were to blame for many of Germany's problems. Art and music were also used to show how wonderful the Germans and the Nazis were.

Propaganda – young people

In school, children were taught all the things that were shown in the posters, in newspapers and on the radio. They were taught that the Nazis were the best thing that had ever happened to Germany. Boys joined the German Young People at 10. Then between 14 and 18 they joined the **Hitler Youth** and did some army training. Girls had separate youth groups.

A painting by the Mexican artist, Diego Rivera, in 1933 It shows Hitler as a ruler who used violence and brutality. Such a painting would not have been allowed in Germany.

In the next issue there must be an article in which the decision of the Führer will be discussed as the only correct one for Germany.

What the press were told by the Ministry of Propaganda just before the Second World War.

Q SOURCE

A Nazi poster from 1933, encouraging young people to join the Hitler Youth Movement.

R SOURCE

A Nazi Party rally in the 1930s.

S SOURCE

A Nazi poster showing the ideal family of four children.

Propaganda – women

The Nazis felt that women should stay at home and be mothers. One strong reason for this was so that they would breed plenty of sons so Germany could have a big army. Women who had large families could win a medal called the Motherhood Cross.

Propaganda – big rallies

The Nazis knew how much people enjoyed a big get together. They organized huge rallies where lots of German soldiers marched, sometimes in torchlight parades. These rallies made a great **spectacle**. German people could feel very proud to see their huge, beautifully turned out army.

In 1936 the Olympic Games were held in Berlin. This was a chance for Hitler to show how superior the Aryan Germans were. Unfortunately for him, the outstanding athlete was a black American called Jesse Owens.

Popularity – peace, strength and who's to blame

In 1933 Germany had been in a mess. Many people had been afraid of a communist revolution. Hitler destroyed communism and brought about a strong government. He built up the army. He got back land Germany had lost after the First World War (see Unit 3.4). He even gave the German people a scapegoat, meaning that all the bad things that had happened to Germany were someone else's fault. Hitler said that losing the war, having no jobs and no savings were the fault of the Jews, the communists and the government just after the First World War.

Popularity – jobs

The most solid thing Hitler gave the Germans, however, was jobs. In 1933 unemployment was six million. In 1938 unemployment was half a million.

How Hitler created jobs:

- Made the army bigger.
- Built roads, schools and railways.
- Made more armaments.

T

SOURCE

5 Mark die Woche musst Du sparen – willst Du im eignen Wagen fahren!

KdF-Wagen: Über Anschaffungspreis und Zahlungsweise erteilen Auskunft alle Betriebswarte und Dienststellen der NS.-Gemeinschaft „Kraft durch Freude" Gau München-Oberbayern

A poster of 1938 encouraging German workers to 'Save five marks a week and get your own car'. The Volkswagen ('people's car') was introduced by the Nazis.

U

SOURCE

The building of roads helped other industries. Workers who built them spent their wages in shops and cafes. The roads also helped the German motor industry. This in turn helped the growth of the electrical industries.

From Norman Stone, 'Hitler', 1980.

Postscript

The Germans had more jobs and more money. The government told the Germans only what the Nazis wanted them to know. It was no wonder that many Germans supported the Nazis. Anyone who spoke out against the Nazis went to prison. So Hitler stayed in power until 1945 when Germany lost the war.

V

SOURCE

A Strength through Joy poster from the 1930s. It is promising workers homes on new housing estates.

W

SOURCE

Whatever one thinks of Hitler's methods... there can be no doubt that he has achieved a marvellous change in the spirit of the people. The old trust him, the young idolize him.

From an article, written in 1936, by David Lloyd George, former British Prime Minister, after he had visited Germany.

Questions

1 Read **How did Hitler stay in power 1933–39**.
What three things did Hitler use so that he could stay as leader?

2 Which sources on pages 46–51 show the way in which Nazis made use of 'spectacle'. Explain your answer.

3 Read Sources K and P. In what ways do these sources show Hitler was all powerful?

4 'Source O is very frightening'. Do you agree?

4.1 War in Western Europe 1939–41

Poland and Blitzkrieg

The Germans attacked Poland. They bombed the Polish cities. Then the German tanks and soldiers moved in. On 24 September, 1,150 German planes bombed the city of Warsaw. The USSR attacked Poland too. The Poles did not have a chance. Germany and the USSR divided Poland between them.

Britain and France get ready

Both Britain and France got ready for war. In Britain the government gave out gas masks and sent many of the children away from the cities. A **blackout** was ordered (blacking out windows and not using lights outside at night) so that German bombers could not see any lights from the air. In France, trains took thousands of people away from the area around the Maginot Line (see map). At the same time other trains took thousands of soldiers up to the Maginot Line.

Phoney war, real war

However, for months no bombers or German soldiers came. This lack of fighting made people call this the Phoney War. It did not last. In April 1940, Germany invaded Norway and Denmark. Then in May, the German Panzer tank units crashed through the forests of the Ardennes and on into France.

The German invasion of France, May 1940.

SOURCE

A

A painting done at the time, showing the rescue of the soldiers from the Dunkirk beaches.

Date	Figures given by RAF in 1940	Figures given by RAF after war	Figures in German High Command Diary
15 August	185	76	55
18 August	155	71	49
15 September	185	56	50
27 September	153	55	42
Totals	678	258	196

Numbers of German aircraft shot down on four days during the Battle of Britain.

French and British on the run

The British sent soldiers to help the French but soon 300,000 French and British soldiers were on the run. The Germans chased them to the port of Dunkirk. It looked as though they would all be killed or taken prisoner.

Dunkirk

The British decided to rescue as many soldiers as possible. They asked for help to get them off the beaches. Between 24 May and 4 June, hundreds of boats from fishing boats to ferries sailed across to France. The smallest boats sailed right up close to the beaches. The soldiers left their coats, held their rifles above their heads and waded out to the small boats. The small boats then took them to the big Royal Naval ships about a mile out to sea. Most of the thousands of soldiers were brought safely back to Britain. They could fight another day.

Would Germany invade Britain?

France surrendered and Germany took over most of France for the rest of the war. But would Germany invade Britain? Hitler knew he had to use his German airforce (the Luftwaffe) to destroy the British airforce (RAF) first. So a fierce battle went on in the skies over southern Britain all through the summer of 1940. Britain just managed to keep the German fighter planes out and by the end of the summer, Hitler gave up his plan to invade Britain. Instead he decided to bomb British factories and cities. He wanted to destroy the factories that made guns, warplanes and so on. He also wanted to frighten British people so that they would surrender. This bombing was called the **Blitz**.

Questions

1 Read **Poland and Blitzkrieg**.
Fill in the gaps.
The Germans attacked _____.
First they bombed the _____,
then the soldiers moved in.

2 Look at the map on page 52.
   a What do the red arrows mean?
   b What town did the Germans chase the British to?

3 Look at Source A.
   a How did the British rescue their army?
   b Find at least two signs of the Germans attacking.

4 Look at Source B.
Which of the three different sets of figures of German planes shot down is most likely to be right? Why?

4.2 The German Invasion of the USSR

Germany and the USSR

Germany and the USSR had signed a pact (see page 38) but Hitler did not like the USSR and wanted some of its land.

Hitler invades the USSR

In June 1941 German soldiers poured into the USSR, speeding across the open spaces. The Soviet soldiers retreated and retreated. By November the German soldiers were deep into the USSR (see map). But the Germans were not prepared for the terrible Soviet winter. Oil froze in the tanks, rubber tyres froze and the soldiers froze too. Many of them only had summer uniforms. Sometimes they almost froze to death. The German soldiers dug trenches and waited in them for spring. It was difficult to get food because the Soviets had burnt all the farms and food as they retreated.

How the Soviets coped

The Soviets moved all their factories hundreds of miles to the east so they would be safe from the Germans. These factories poured out guns and other weapons as fast as possible. In one factory the big guns were loaded on to the trains unpainted. Women workers went on the trains painting the guns while the trains slowly made their way across the countryside to the Soviet soldiers at the front.

Spring and Stalingrad

After the winter the German soldiers continued to advance. They wanted to capture the oilfields in the Caucasus (see map). The Germans reached the city of Stalingrad but the Soviets were determined to stop them there. They fought street by street to keep their city from the Germans.

A

SOURCE

A German soldier using a flame-thrower to attack a Soviet village.

B

Rifles got so cold that if a man picked his up with his bare hand, the hand stuck to the rifle. It was so cold that he didn't realize what had happened. When he took his hand away the flesh of his palm and his fingers stayed on the rifle.

SOURCE

From R. Seth, 'Operation Barbarossa', 1964.

Winter and Stalingrad

The fighting went on for months. In November more Soviet soldiers arrived and surrounded the Germans. Hitler said the Germans must fight on. But the German General, Von Paulus, said it was hopeless. He surrendered to the Soviets in February 1943.

Result

The Germans lost about 200,000 soldiers. The Soviets lost about 20,000,000 soldiers and civilians. These were terrible losses for the USSR, but the Germans had been driven back. The USSR had not been taken over by the Germans. The Germans had been beaten for the first time.

C

SOURCE

A Soviet cartoon showing Hitler ordering his soldiers to their death.

The German attack on the USSR, 1941–2.

N

⟶ German advance, June 1941 to December 1942

⟶ Furthest extent of German advances, December 1942

⟶ Russian advances after 1942

0 — 300 miles
0 — 400 km

Baltic Sea

Leningrad

Moscow

Smolensk

POLAND

Kiev

Stalingrad

SLOVAKIA

HUNGARY

CAUCASUS

ROMANIA

Black Sea

Questions

1 Read the first paragraph.
   a What was the pact the USSR and Germany had signed?
   b Did Hitler like the USSR?
   c What did Hitler want?

2 Look at Source C. Write a sentence to explain how the artist shows that the soldiers are going to their deaths.

3 Read Source B. Does it agree or disagree with Source C? Why do you think this?

4.3 *E*urope under the Nazis

By the end of 1942 Germany controlled most of Europe. The only countries that stood against Hitler were the USSR and Britain.

What Germany got

As soon as German soldiers had conquered a country, they took everything they could. They took food, coal, oil, shoes, machines, art treasures and clothes. For instance, France was famous for beautiful clothes. When the Germans conquered France they sent train loads of French silk stockings back to Germany. For a while the German shops were full of silk stockings.

Slave workers

People were taken too. Germany needed millions of people to work on farms. By 1944 there were seven million slave workers in Germany. Many of these were from the USSR.

SOURCE

The starving Soviet [Russian] prisoners passed in endless columns. Those who could not keep up were shot. We spent the night in a small village and saw how, at night, the prisoners roasted and ate those of their fellows who had been shot.

From Fiona Reynoldson, 'Prisoners of War', 1990. Quote by Dr Faulhaber.

Europe at the end of 1942.

Western Europe

The Germans treated the people of western Europe quite well. In Norway and France they let local men rule. However the Germans used the Gestapo (secret police) and the SS (Schutzstaffel – Hitler's own army) to make sure that everyone obeyed. The local men were only allowed to run the country as long as they ran it in the right way.

Eastern Europe

The people who supported the Nazis in Germany looked down on the USSR, Poland and all the other countries that Germany had conquered. They killed thousands of these people. In some parts of the USSR it is estimated that the Nazis killed at least one person out of every four people. No one knows for sure. Whole villages were burnt. The Nazis wanted the land cleared so that German people could farm it.

Questions

1 Read **What Germany got**. Make a list of the things that Germany took from other countries.

2 Look at the map on page 56. Make a list of the countries that Germany took over.

3 Read **Eastern Europe**. Choose the two reasons that best explain why the Germans treated the Soviets badly:
The Germans were cleverer.
The Germans wanted the land.
The Germans looked down on the Soviets.
The Germans were careless.

German soldiers hanging Soviet people.

SOURCE

B

4.4 Opposition to the Nazis

How the Germans felt about Hitler

At first Hitler was popular in Germany. He had made Germany rich and great again. He had made lots of jobs for Germans. Most people closed their eyes to other things that Hitler did, like getting rid of trade unions and persecuting Jews.

What happened to people who didn't like the Nazis?

Some Germans spoke out. They said that Hitler should not harm the Jews or anyone else. Hitler did not tolerate this. Anyone who spoke against him was arrested and often killed.

Resistance

In the countries that the Germans had conquered many people hated the Nazi rule. Some of these people carried on a secret war against the Germans. They were called the Resistance. They did as much as they could to fight the Nazis. They put bombs on railway lines, so that German soldiers and goods could not be moved so easily. They printed secret newspapers with lots of stories against the Germans. They helped Jews and others to escape. There were resistance groups like this in France, Poland and other countries.

Anyone caught resisting the Germans was killed. Sometimes his or her whole family or even the whole village was killed too.

SOURCE A

Dear Parents: bad news, I have been condemned to death. Gustav and I did not sign up for the SS. Both of us would rather die. I know what the SS have to do. We do not want to do it.

Written by a German farm worker in prison.

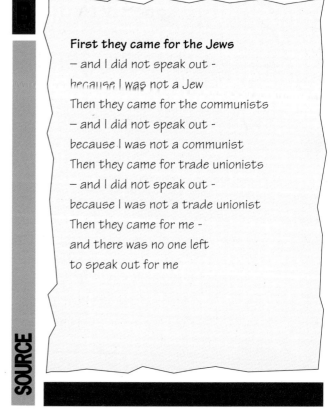

SOURCE B

First they came for the Jews
– and I did not speak out -
because I was not a Jew
Then they came for the communists
– and I did not speak out -
because I was not a communist
Then they came for trade unionists
– and I did not speak out -
because I was not a trade unionist
Then they came for me -
and there was no one left
to speak out for me

A poem written in prison by Pastor Niemoller, a German churchman.

C

SOURCE

A woman taking a secret photograph. She is pretending to look for something in her bag. The lens of the hidden camera is just below the centre of the two rings of the bag.

D

SOURCE

We helped some Soviet prisoners to escape. Poor people. They were forced to clear mines (bombs) from the minefield by walking in a line with linked arms over the field.

From S. Saywell, 'Women at War', 1985. Said by Carla Capponi.

The Allies and the Resistance

The Allies wanted to defeat Germany. So they helped the Resistance in places like France. In 1940, Britain formed a **Special Operations Executive** (SOE). The SOE trained men and women to go secretly into countries that the Germans had taken over to help the Resistance in those places. One way they could help was to find out where the big guns were, or where lots of soldiers were. All the information that they collected helped the Allies when they invaded Europe on D-Day.

Questions

1 Read the first and second paragraphs. Fill in the gaps. Hitler was popular in _____. He had made lots of _____. People tried to forget that he also persecuted _____. The Germans who spoke against him, were _____ or killed.

2 Read Source B. Choose the sentence which best describes what it means:
You should not interfere.
You should always think of yourself first.
You should speak out for what is right.

4.5 War in the Pacific

The war spreads

By the end of 1941 the Second World War had spread across the world to the Pacific Ocean (the Far East).

Japan and the Far East

Europeans and Americans made lots of money trading with countries in the Far East. For instance, Britain and the USA got most of their rubber from Malaya. They made lots of money in the trade. Japan said this was unfair. However, Japan was not interested in the people of Malaya making money. Japan was more interested in making money itself. Japan wanted to control the Far East, all around the Pacific Ocean.

Japan and the USA

The USA did not want Japan to control the Far East. So the USA refused to sell any oil to Japan. This was a disaster. Japan got 80% of its oil from the USA. How could Japan run machines and factories? How could Japan make any trucks, tanks, bicycles or other machines at all?

1941

Japan decided to take land in the Far East. For instance, there was oil in the Philippines (see map). But the Japanese had to be careful. They had to be sure that the Americans did not use the American navy to stop them taking places like the Philippines. So Japan decided to knock out the American navy.

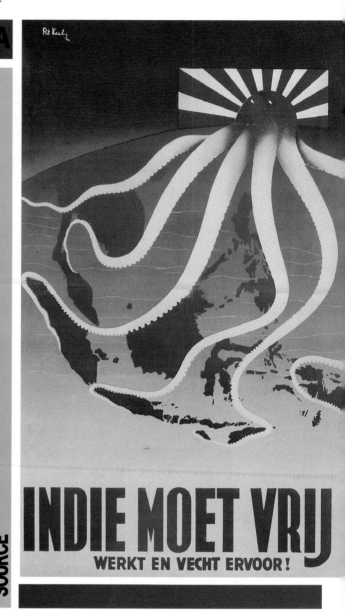

A

SOURCE

INDIE MOET VRIJ
WERKT EN VECHT ERVOOR!

A Dutch poster from the time. Before the war the Dutch had owned many of the islands shown on this poster.

Pearl Harbor

The night of 6 December was beautiful. It was Saturday night and everyone at the American navy base of **Pearl Harbor** was looking forward to a fine Sunday. Many of the big American ships were anchored in the harbour. None of the American soldiers or sailors knew that the huge Japanese fleet was only 200 miles away. It was sitting silently in the moonlight waiting for dawn.

At 7.53 am next morning the first Japanese planes swooped on Pearl Harbor. They blew up ships and planes and killed over 2000 people. The Americans were angry and scared. The only good thing was that the big American aircraft carriers were at sea at the time of the attack so they were quite safe.

Results

The Japanese had won for the moment. They went on to take more and more islands in the Far East. These included the British base at Singapore (see map).

The war in the Pacific, 1941–2.

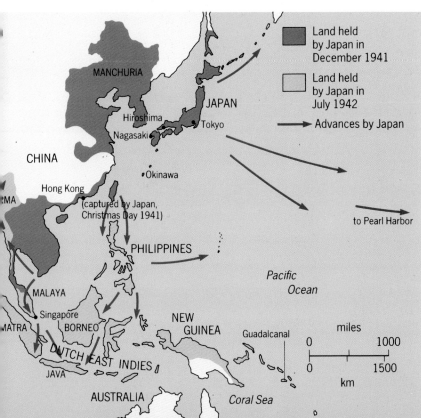

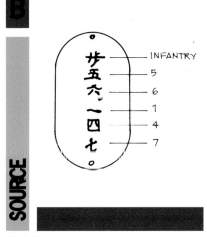

Soldiers of every army wore identity discs. Sometimes it was the only thing left when a soldier was killed. This Japanese soldier was in unit 56 and his own number was 147.

Questions

1 Read **Japan and the Far East**. Copy the following sentences. Use one of the words in *italics* each time there is a choice. *Americans/Africans* and many Europeans made money trading in the Far East. Japan wanted to make *money/honey* itself. Japan wanted to control the *Near/Far* East.

2 Look at Source A. The red and white flag is Japanese.
   a What animal is Japan shown as?
   b Who made the poster?
   c Do you think they liked the Japanese? Explain why you think this.

4.6 The Allied Victories in the West

By 1942 the Allies were made up of the USA, Britain, France and the USSR. Now they were stronger than Germany. They started to win.

North Africa

The Suez Canal and the Mediterranean Sea were important to Britain. They were the way to the oil fields in the Middle East. Britain fought Germany and Italy to stop them getting to the Suez Canal. The British won at the Battle of El Alamein. From then on the British and the Americans worked together to push the German armies back.

The USSR

From 1942 the Soviets pushed the German armies back (see map on page 63).

France and D-Day, 6 June 1944

The Americans and the British sent thousands of soldiers to fight the Germans in France. They used 7,000 ships and landed 156,000 soldiers on the beaches on the first day (called D-Day). Someone said it was like moving the whole of a big city like Birmingham to France in one day. Every soldier had enough food for 24 hours. He carried everything from chewing gum to stop him feeling seasick, to spare socks and a rifle.

The soldiers fought the Germans and captured the beaches. Then more and more American and British soldiers were landed on the beaches. They fought their way inland. By September there were two million soldiers in France. Slowly, very slowly, they pushed the German soldiers back towards Germany (see map).

A SOURCE

In German cities people camped in the ruins with no light, heat or water, and had to scavenge like animals.

From S. L. Case, 'The Second World War', 1981.

B SOURCE

ВПЕРЕД, НА ЗАПАД!

A Soviet poster, encouraging their soldiers to fight the Germans.

Bombing

The British and the Americans bombed German cities. They sent as many as 1,000 bombers at a time. German cities like Dresden, Hamburg and Cologne were flattened. By May 1945, whole streets in Berlin were a mass of rubble and bricks. Many died in the bombing and in the fires which were so powerful they sucked people into the flames. Survivors lived in the cellars.

The end of the war in the West

In May 1945, the Soviets reached Berlin from the east. The British, Americans and French reached Berlin from the west (see map). Hitler killed himself and Germany surrendered.

Questions

1 Read the first paragraph. Who were the Allies?

2 Look at the map on this page.
   a What are the red arrows?
   b What are the purple arrows?

3 Look at Source B
   a Who made this poster?
   b Choose a word from below to say how the soldier feels.

> happy sad fierce desperate determined calm brave

The defeat of Germany.

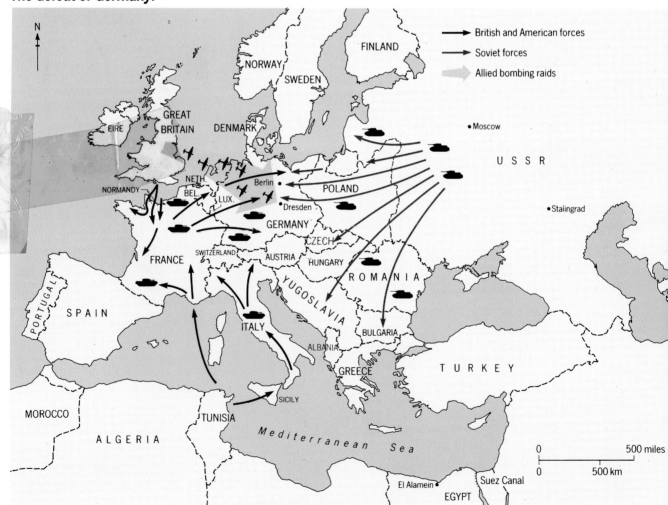

4.7 Victory in the Pacific

In 1942 Japan held lots of land in the Far East. But the USA was fighting back. The American navy won sea battles at Coral Sea and Midway.

Soldiers and kamikazes

The USA decided to capture one island at a time. Each time they got a little nearer to Japan. The Japanese fought very hard. Japanese people thought it was dreadful to surrender. If a Japanese soldier surrendered his family would not be given a pension.

On the other hand to die for Japan was a great honour. Young men queued up to be trained as suicide or kamikaze pilots. They flew planes loaded with bombs straight into the American and British ships. All the bombs blew up and the ships blew up as well.

The USA fights towards Japan

As 1943 and 1944 went by American soldiers got nearer and nearer to Japan. By mid 1945 the Japanese were in a desperate position. American bombers dropped fire bombs on cities like Tokyo. Thousands died.

D

SOURCE

The city of Hiroshima after the atomic bomb had been dropped.

Would Japan surrender?

The Japanese thought of surrendering, but did not do so. The Americans wanted to make sure Japan was completely defeated and could not fight again. The Americans planned to invade Japan. But they knew the Japanese would fight to the death. The American government was worried that the American people would be against invading Japan because of this. How many of their soldiers would die?

The atomic bomb

The answer to the problem seemed to be the new atomic bomb. It was very powerful. No one really knew just how powerful it would be. It was top secret.

The American President sent a message to the Japanese. They must give up everything to the Americans. The Japanese did not reply.

Hiroshima

On the morning of 6 August 1945, an American bomber flew over the city of Hiroshima and dropped the very first atomic bomb. A huge mushroom cloud rose into the sunny sky. The bomber turned away. Below it the city of Hiroshima lay in ruins.

Nagasaki

The Japanese still would not surrender so the Americans dropped another atomic bomb, this time on Nagasaki. The Soviets attacked in the north. Now the Japanese gave up. The war was over.

My daughter had no burns. But then, on 4 September she got very sick. Her hair began to fall out, and she vomited clots of blood many times. After ten days of agony she died.

Said by a father in Hiroshima about his daughter's death.

Questions

1 Read the first paragraph. Copy the following sentences. Choose one of the words in *italics* when there is a choice.
In 1942 Japan had lots of *land/elephants* in the Far East. Then the USA started to win some famous *land/sea/air* battles. One of these was the Battle of *Halfway/Midway*.

2 Read **The USA fights towards Japan** and **Would Japan surrender?**.
   a Who was in a bad position by 1945?
   b What did the Japanese think of doing?
   c What did the Americans want to be sure of?

3 Look at Source D. Read Sources B and C.
Which source do you agree with? Why do you think this?

4.8 The Holocaust

Aryan people

Hitler said that Germans and other people in north Europe were Aryans. He said Aryans were the master race. They should rule the world.

Jews

Hitler and the Nazi Party hated anyone who was not Aryan. They hated the Jews most of all. Hitler said that the Jews were to blame for everything bad that happened. Then he said that the Jews were also to blame for everything bad that had ever happened to Germany in the past. He went on and on in his speeches about how bad the Jews were until, in the end, many ordinary Germans began to believe the things he said about the Jews.

Shops, jobs and public places

Nazi soldiers smashed Jewish shop windows. Jews got beaten up by soldiers more and more often. Then, in 1933, all Jews were thrown out of government jobs.

Worse and worse

In 1935 Jews were banned from using public swimming pools and parks. Non-Jews were not allowed to marry Jews. Things got worse and worse. Hitler and the Nazis began to pick on people who were only partly Jewish. People who were half or a quarter Jewish were told they were Jews. Many people found out that their grandmother or great-grandfather had been Jewish. They were terrified.

A SOURCE

A Nazi poster, showing the Germans clearing out the 'muck' – communists and Jews.

B

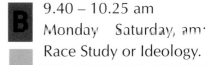

9.40 – 10.25 am
Monday Saturday, am
Race Study or Ideology.

From a German school timetable in the Nazi period.

C SOURCE

When I went to school, aged 10, a third of my classmates were Jewish girls. I got on just as well with them as with the other girls. But we were told that the Jews were all wicked.

Said by a German woman who went to school in the Nazi period.

9 November 1938

On 9 November 1938 a German was murdered in Paris, and a Jew was blamed. The Nazi Party sent soldiers to punish all the Jews they could find. The soldiers burnt homes and synagogues (places where Jewish people worship) and smashed shops.

Concentration camps

Over 30,000 Jews were sent to concentration camps. These were prison camps for people who the Nazis did not like. The Jews joined everyone else who Hitler disliked, or who had stood up to him. After this many Jews ran away from Germany.

E **SOURCE** In 1934 a schoolboy in Berlin said, 'My Daddy says that not all Jews are vile.' His daddy was put in prison.

From T. Howarth, 'The World Since 1914', 1979.

Questions

1 Read the first paragraph. What was the name that Hitler gave the 'master race'?

2 Read **Jews**. Choose the sentence which best explains how Hitler got so many Germans to believe the Jews were bad:
Hitler kept quiet about Jews.
Hitler wrote 20 books.
Hitler kept on saying that the Jews were bad.

3 Look at Source D.
   a What does the picture the boy is pointing to show?
   b What does Source D tell you about Nazi schools?

4 Look at Source A.
Why do you think the Nazis made this poster?

D **SOURCE**

A cartoon showing an anti-Jewish lesson. The pupils are being taught what were seen as signs of Jewishness.

Ghettoes and concentration camps

The Germans treated the Jews badly in each country they conquered. Sometimes Jews were shut up in separate places inside cities (**ghettoes**). Often the Jewish children, women and men starved. Other Jews were sent to concentration camps where they were put to work. They were often worked to death.

The Holocaust

Hitler decided on a **Final Solution** to the Jewish 'problem'. It meant killing all the Jews. It has become known as the Holocaust.

Six million Jews were killed. Some were shot but this was too slow for the Nazis. They built big halls (chambers) at some camps. They sent up to 2,000 Jews into them. Sometimes they gave each person a bar of stone which they said was soap. The Jews thought they were going for a wash. They went into the chamber. The doors were sealed. Gas was put into it. In three minutes everyone was dead. The bodies were burned.

Experiments

At other camps Jews were used for medical experiments, often without **anaesthetics**. Most of them died.

The main concentration camps.

The end of the war

When the Allied soldiers saw the concentration camps they were horrified. They vomitted at what they saw. They took photographs and films to show all the world what had happened to stop it ever happening again.

Rows of corpses waiting to be buried at a Nazi death camp.

I

It is the greatest mass killing in history, and it goes on daily, hourly. I have been talking to Allied troops about this for three years now, and it is always the same. They don't believe it.

Written by A. Koestler, and American journalist, in the 'New York Times', 1944.

Questions

1 Read **The Holocaust**. Fill in the gaps.
The Holocaust was the killing of _____ million Jews by the Nazis. Some were _____. Others were herded into _____ and gassed.

2 Read Source G. The writer was a Nazi. Choose the sentence which best explains why he was still shocked by what he saw:
He was a kind man.
He was a weak person.
He was seeing the gassing for the first time.
He was lying in the 1960s.

3 Read **Experiments**.
How did the Nazis feel about the people they did this to?

The Second World War was total war. For the first time bombers could fly far into enemy lands and bomb factories and cities.

The Blitz

In September 1940 Hitler gave up his plans to invade Britain. He decided to bomb the cities instead.

The big bombers

The bombing started on 7 September and went on for months. Night after night people heard the wail of the air raid siren. Then they heard the throb of the bombers' engines. Dogs howled. Small fire bombs clattered on roofs. Big bombs sounded like tearing sheets. Then came the crash of houses blowing up; the thud of walls falling down, the sound of fire alarms and the crackle of flames. Added to this was the hard ack-ack noise of the anti-aircraft guns as they tried to blow the German bombers out of the sky.

Blackout, sirens and shelters

The government ordered a blackout. No street lights – and not even lighting a cigarette in the street. (Some people did wonder whether pilots could really see a lighted cigarette from an aeroplane!) Air raid sirens were put on top of buildings and wailed their warnings as German bombers were spotted. People built air-raid shelters in their gardens or hid under tables indoors.

B SOURCE

The warden shouted, 'Get in your shelters.' I can't remember the sound, just the tumbling walls, the dust, and then the night sky. Our house had vanished.

Told to Fiona Reynoldson by Gerald Cole.

A SOURCE

How much sleep did you get last night?

| None 31% | Less than 4 hours 32% | 4–6 hours 22% | More than 6 hours 15% |

SOURCE

A bus in a bomb crater in London in 1940.

SOURCE

The centre of Canterbury after heavy bombing.

Questions

1 Read **The Blitz**.
   a What did Hitler give up in September 1940?
   b What did he decide to do instead?

2 Read **Blackouts, sirens and shelters**.
   Write a sentence about each of the above.

3 'Sources C and D show that the bombing brought life to a stand still.' Do you agree with this statement?

D

SOURCE

People who have lived here all their lives don't know the way outside their doorsteps. I've never seen a place so beat – there's not a thing working.

A 'Mass Observation' report on Southampton in 1941. Mass Observation was set up to study how British people lived.

From Blitz to Atomic Wipeout

About 40,000 people died in the air-raids on London, Coventry, Glasgow and other British cities. In 1942 Britain decided to bomb German cities. Some people were upset by the thought of bombing ordinary civilians but they thought it was more important to win the war than worry about that. It is difficult to know how much bombing helped in winning the war. It certainly did not break people's will to keep on fighting the enemy even when the bombing went on night after night.

Victims of allied bombing in Dresden, February 1945.

The USA and Japan

The US airforce bombed Japanese cities to rubble. Then they were faced with a very difficult decision. The USA had made a very powerul bomb. It was known as the **atomic bomb**. If they dropped the atomic bomb on a Japanese city it would kill so many people that Japan would surrender. This would save thousands of American soldiers' lives. But the USA knew the atomic bomb was the most terrifying bomb ever made and would cause dreadful harm. In the end the USA decided to use the bomb and dropped two bombs on Hiroshima and Nagasaki in August 1945.

Dresden has become the main centre of communications defence of Germany. It has never been bombed before. And, as a large centre of war industry, it is very important.

Sir Arthur Harris, who was in charge of the British Bomber Command (1942–45).

Bombs dropped on Britain and Germany 1940–45 (in tons)		
Year	Britain	Germany
1940	37,000	10,000
1941	21,000	30,000
1942	3,000	40,000
1943	9,000	120,000
1944	2,000	650,000
1945	750	500,000

Bombing during the Second World War.

It struck me at the time, the thought of women and children down there. We seemed to fly for hours over a sheet of fire – a terrific red glow. You can't justify it.

The views of an RAF pilot who took part in the bombing of Dresden.

H

SOURCE

Stacked up corpses were being hauled away on lorries. I saw places on the pavement where people had been roasted to death. At last I understood what an air-raid meant.

Memories of a Japanese girl who experienced the bombing raids on Tokyo in March 1945.

I

The impact of the bomb was so terrific that practically all living things were seared to death by the heat and pressure of the blast.

Radio Tokyo after the atomic bombing of Hiroshima in Japan.

J

SOURCE

The engineering director of the atomic project was desperate to see if it worked. Since it had cost 2,000 million dollars to develop the bomb, it was difficult not to use it. However, the scientists failed to say anything about the long term dangers of radiation. In a way, the dropping of the atomic bombs was an experiment.

From an article in the magazine of the Campaign for Nuclear Disarmament published in 1985.

K

SOURCE

All of us realized that it might cost half a million American lives to make Japan surrender. I had realized that an atomic bomb explosion would cause damage beyond imagination. I talked to the British Prime Minister, Churchill, and he told me he favoured the use of the bomb if it would help to shorten the war.

From the memoirs of President Truman, who ordered the dropping of atomic bombs on Hiroshima and Nagasaki.

Questions

1 Look at the figures of bombs dropped on Britain and Germany.
   a In what year did Britain start to drop more bombs on Germany than the other way round?
   b Look at Sources C, D and E as well as the figures. How severe was the bombing of Britain in the war?

2 Read Sources F and G.
   a Which source is in favour of bombing?
   b Which source is against bombing?
   c How did one of them justify the bombing?

3 Read Source K.
   a Why do you think President Truman favoured using the atomic bomb?
   b What doubts did he have about it?
   c How did Churchill justify using the atomic bomb, according to Truman?

Getting away from the bombs

All the fighting countries tried to get their children away from the bombs. At the beginning of the war, the French moved thousands away from their border with Germany. Germany did the same. The British, fearing bombing, moved three million children and some adults out of the cities to safer places. At the end of the war both the Japanese and Germans were fleeing from bombed cities and advancing armies.

Leaving British cities – evacuation September 1939

School children left the cities with their schools. Children under five went with their mothers. Hundreds of trains took the children to the country. Each train carried about 800 children. None of them knew where they were going. The children were met at stations and local people took them to their homes. Some children settled down happily. Many did not. The country people had to put up with a lot too. They took strange children into their homes. No bombs fell at first so by Christmas nine out of ten children went home. Later, when the bombs came, many children did not leave the cities again.

M
SOURCE

A government poster from the Second World War.

L
SOURCE

This drawing shows children leaving a big city.

N
SOURCE

Everything was so clean. We were given toothbrushes. We'd never cleaned our teeth until then. And the hot water came from a tap. And there was a toilet upstairs. And carpets. This was all very odd. I didn't like it.

Memories of a Second World War evacuee.

O

SOURCE

This drawing shows children arriving in the country.

Q

SOURCE

I looked out of the window and I saw my mother crying outside. I said to my brother, 'Why is mummy crying?' He told me to shut up.

Memories of a Second World War evacuee.

P

SOURCE

Children on their way to the countryside, 1938.

Questions

1 Read **Getting away from the bombs**. Fill in the gaps.
All the fighting countries tried to get their —— away from the ——. The British, fearing bombing, moved —— million children and some adults out of the ——.

2 Look at Sources L and O. Write a sentence for each picture to explain what is happening.

3 Look at Source P.
   a Choose one word from the list below which you think best describes how the children feel.

   > sad happy upset
   > worried lost scared
   > frightened OK

   b Do you think Source N is more or less reliable than Source P? Explain your answer.

War changes everything

Bombing and evacuating children to safe places meant many changes in family life. Another change happened because many men between the ages of 18 and 41 went to fight.

Women and war

The war changed women's lives greatly. Often the men of the family were away. Women were running the family and often doing a job on their own.

Running the family and rationing

Most of Britain's food came from other countries by ship. During the war many ships were sunk. So Britain was short of food. Food was rationed (shared out among everyone). Everyone in Britain had a ration card. This was very fair. But mothers now had to cope with rationing. They had to make a little food do lots of meals. Sometimes there was so little food that women had to queue for hours to get one piece of fish.

Women out at work

The government wanted women to work in the factories and on the farms. In 1940 all women under 50 years of age

S

SOURCE

One person's rations for one week.

T

Most people are better fed than they used to be. Rationing has increased the amount of milk that people drink.

SOURCE

George Orwell talking about rationing at the time.

R

SOURCE

A wartime painting of a woman doing a skilled job using complicated machines.

76

had to go out to work (unless their children were under 14 years old).

Farms

By 1943 there were nearly 80,000 women in the Women's Land Army to do the work of the men who had gone to war. They drove tractors, milked cows, planted potatoes and dug ditches.

Factories

Many women worked in factories. They were always paid less than men for the same job, but many had their own money for the first time in their lives. They liked it. Some women at factories like Rolls Royce went on strike for equal pay. They said that women doing skilled work on the machines were only paid the same as unskilled men who cleaned the lavatories. Was this fair? At last the women got paid more money (but not as much as the skilled men).

Women's Voluntary Service

Older women often joined the WVS. These women did everything from driving ambulances, running canteens at railway stations to collecting metal to make aeroplanes.

Dad's Army (the Home Guard)

Older men often joined the Home Guard. After work they went off to train as soldiers in case Britain was invaded. When they weren't doing that they were digging their gardens to grow as many vegetables as possible to feed the family.

SOURCE U

Wartime women on a protest march.

Questions

1 Read **Running the family and rationing**. Match the Heads and Tails.

Heads	Tails
Women queued for hours	by ship.
Every person in Britain	sunk.
Most of Britain's food came	had a ration card.
Food was shared out among	for a piece of fish.
Many ships were	short of food.
Britain was	everyone.

2 Look at Source S. List how much of each thing you could have then. List what you eat in a day now.
   a How much more or less than the rations do you eat now?
   b What else do you eat?
   c How much of this comes from other countries (probably by ship)?

What is propaganda?

Propaganda is a sort of advertising. Advertisements on television or in magazines tell us what to buy. In wartime, governments use propaganda to tell us what to do. Governments sell the war as a good idea. Then everyone will fight hard. Propaganda can be a leaflet, poster, newspaper story, a film or on radio.

Soviet propaganda

Everyone used propaganda in the war. For instance, the Soviet government wanted all the Soviet people to fight the Germans. They made a postcard of Hitler as a gorilla behind bars and sent thousands of these postcards to all the soldiers fighting.

SOURCE V

13·MÄRZ 1938
EIN VOLK EIN REICH
EIN FÜHRER

A Nazi poster of Hitler. It says 'One people, one empire, one leader'.

British propaganda

At the beginning of the war the British dropped twelve million leaflets from aeroplanes which flew over Germany. The leaflets were written in German. They told the Germans how bad the war would be for them. They should give up now.

Radio and cinema

All the sides fighting made radio broadcasts. They said how good their side was or how bad the other side was. They all made films too. The films made their side look very brave. They made the other side look very bad.

SOURCE W

During a war news must be carefully controlled. Some news should not be made public.

From the diaries of Joseph Goebbels, Hitler's minister of propaganda.

TYPES OF PROPAGANDA IN THE WAR

To keep their own people cheerful, and to depress the enemy, both sides changed the way they reported things. The type of propaganda they used varied.

The same report can be given in three different ways:

WHITE PROPAGANDA (The True Story):
We fought a tough battle on Tuesday. Both sides lost about 5,000 men. We only just won.

GREY PROPAGANDA (Half Truths):
We won a victory on Tuesday. We fought hard and finally beat the enemy. It was a long and fierce battle. The enemy lost about 5,000 men.

BLACK PROPAGANDA (Lies):
We beat the enemy again on Tuesday. It was an easy victory. We killed 20,000 of the enemy. Their soldiers ran away. We only lost 50 of our own men.

Y

SOURCE

As well as the BBC the British ran 'black propaganda' stations. They were not concerned with the truth. They pretended to be German radio stations. They told all sorts of lies about the German leaders. [The British wanted to get the Germans to hate their leaders.]

From Fiona Reynoldson, 'Propaganda', 1990.

Z

SOURCE

A Russian poster of Hitler from the Second World War.

Propaganda was used in various ways during the Second World War.

Questions

1 Read **What is propaganda?** Fill in the gaps.
Propaganda is a sort of _____.
Adverts tell us what to _____.
In wartime governments use _____ to tell people what to do. They want to make everyone fight _____.

2 Write down the things from this list which could be used as propaganda.

> posters films flowerpots
> air raids books banks trees
> leaflets burgers radio food

3 Look at Source V carefully. Read the caption.
   a What message is the poster trying to get over?
   b How does the poster do this?

4 Look at Source Z carefully. Read the caption.
   a What message is the poster trying to get over?
   b How does it do this?

5 Look at Source X. Think up some propaganda of your own. Choose something like a pop group. Write a sentence about it. Turn the sentence into white, then grey, then black propaganda.

5.1 A Divided Europe

The division of Europe after 1945.

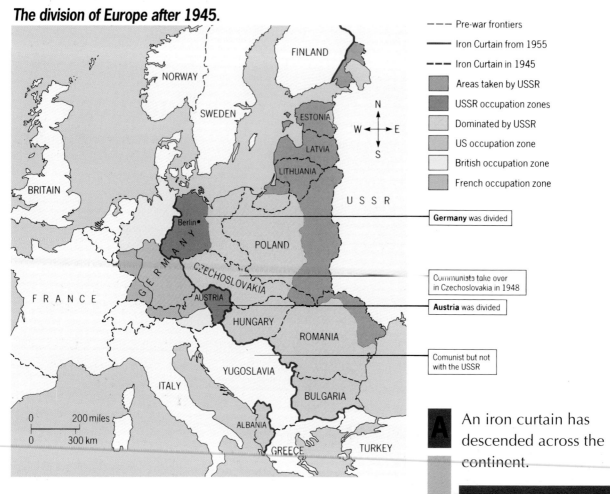

Legend:
- - - - - Pre-war frontiers
- ——— Iron Curtain from 1955
- - - - - Iron Curtain in 1945
- Areas taken by USSR
- USSR occupation zones
- Dominated by USSR
- US occupation zone
- British occupation zone
- French occupation zone

Germany was divided

Communists take over in Czechoslovakia in 1948

Austria was divided

Comunist but not with the USSR

The last German soldiers surrendered on 7 May 1945.

The Allies meet

The Allies were Britain, the USA, France and the USSR. They had won the war. They divided Germany into four **zones**. There was one for each of the Allies (see map). Berlin was Germany's capital city. It was divided into four zones as well.

The Allies argue

The USSR never wanted to be invaded again. So the USSR grabbed as much land as it could. Look at the map on this page. All the mauve and purple land was controlled by the USSR. It made a buffer or block between

A An iron curtain has descended across the continent.

Said by Winston Churchill in a speech in the USA, in 1946.

B As early as 1941 Stalin had made it clear that the USSR would only allow friendly countries on its borders. He said that twice in thirty years the USSR had been invaded through an unfriendly Poland.

SOURCE

From L. Snellgrove, 'The Modern World Since 1870', 1981.

the USSR and Germany. The Soviets said they were taking this land to make themselves safer, not because they were greedy for more land.

The Cold War

Although the USSR had fought on the same side as Britain, France and the USA, the Soviets did not agree about how countries should be run. Britain, France and the USA believed in democracy. The USSR believed in communism. In 1947 **President Truman** of the USA said he did not want to see the USSR controlling any more land and making all the people be communists.

Although there was no fighting between the Allies there was bad feeling. The Soviets were on one side and the Americans, British and French were on the other. This was called the Cold War.

C By 1948 all the countries which the USSR controlled had one-party governments which were controlled by the communists.

SOURCE

From J. Scott, ' The World Since 1914', 1989.

Questions

1 Look at the map on page 80.
   a What colour is the British zone?
   b In whose zone was Berlin?
   c What colour is the line of the Iron Curtain?
   d Who controlled the countries to the east of the Iron Curtain?

2 Read the paragraph **The Cold War**.
   a Is the statement below true or false?
   'The Allies did not fight each other, but there was bad feeling.'
   b The USA, Britain and France were on one side in the Cold War. Which country was on the other side?

D

SOURCE

The court at Nuremberg, where many Nazis were tried for 'war crimes'. Many were never caught or tried.

5.2 The United Nations Organization

Many countries were tired of war. They wanted peace. They wanted fewer guns in the world. They wanted better health for everyone. They wanted everyone to be free.

The United Nations Charter 1945

Just as the war was ending, many countries sent people to the USA. They talked about making a better world. Twenty-six signed the United Nations Charter (Source B).

The General Assembly

A special building was built in New York. It was called the United Nations Building. Men and women from every country that joined met in a big hall in the building. They talked about how they would make the world a better place to live in. When all the members met it was called the **General Assembly**.

B

SOURCE

1 Against war.
2 Defend the worth of all people.
3 Equal rights for men and women and all countries.
4 Respect treaties.
5 Improve world-wide standards of living.

The main beliefs of the United Nations Charter, 1945.

C

SOURCE

The League of Nations thought that all nations would put the good of the world first, before their own interests.

The United Nations accepts that nations are greedy, selfish, and prepared to help others only as long as too much is not demanded of them.

From P. Moss, 'Modern World History', 1978.

THE LEAGUE OF NATIONS | UNITED NATIONS

MANY IMPORTANT COUNTRIES, INCLUDING U.S.A., DID NOT JOIN | EVERY IMPORTANT NATION IS A MEMBER

A NUMBER OF NATIONS WALKED OUT WHEN THEY DID NOT AGREE | THERE IS NO PROVISION FOR A MEMBER TO LEAVE THE U.N. THOUGH MEMBERS MAY BE EXPELLED

THE LEAGUE HAD NO ARMED FORCE TO STOP WAR | MEMBERS PROVIDE SOLDIERS FOR SPECIAL TASKS

A

SOURCE

This cartoon compares the League of Nations with the United Nations. P. Moss, 'History Alive', 1977.

The Security Council

Five important countries were permanent members of the Security Council. These were the USA, Britain, the USSR, China and France. Six other countries (later 10 other countries) sent members to sit on the Security Council for two years at a time. The Security Council met often and ran the United Nations.

The Right to Veto

All the five permanent members had a **veto**. For instance, if they voted on whether to send United Nations' soldiers to keep the peace in Korea and one of the five did not agree, then that one could say no. This no, or veto, meant that the soldiers would not be sent.

Some organizations run by the United Nations

- Court of International Justice
- Food and Agriculture Organization
- United Nations Education, Scientific and Cultural Organization
- World Health Organization
- United Nations Relief and Rehabilitation Administration
- International Refugee Organization

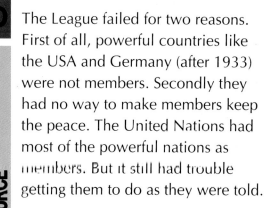

D The League failed for two reasons. First of all, powerful countries like the USA and Germany (after 1933) were not members. Secondly they had no way to make members keep the peace. The United Nations had most of the powerful nations as members. But it still had trouble getting them to do as they were told.

From J Scott, 'The World Since 1914', 1989.

Questions

1 Match the Heads and Tails.

Heads	Tails
Many countries were	to be free.
They wanted everyone	tired of war.
They wanted world	to live well.
They wanted everyone	peace.

2 Read the paragraph **The United Nations Charter**. Read Source B.
  a Write down the main points of the Charter.
  b Design a poster to show what they were.

3 Look at Source A.
  In what three ways was the United Nations better than the League of Nations?

4 Read the last section and Sources B and D.
  a Why might the United Nations have trouble with Point 2 of the Charter?
  b Which organization might help people to reach Point 5 of the Charter?

5.3 Refugees

Refugees are people who have been forced to leave their homes.

The Second World War and refugees

The war was a world war so there were millions of refugees all over the world. Huge armies had fought with guns and tanks over miles and miles of land. Many homes were burnt or blown up. People ran away. Many Jews and others were forced to leave their homes during the war.

The Americans had bombed Japan so much that many Japanese had no homes. In China there were thousands and thousands of women, men and children who had lost their homes in the fighting with Japan.

Europe at the end of the war

Europe was a mess. The Soviets advanced into Germany at the end of the war. Terrified Germans packed their bags and fled to the west. Millions of panic stricken refugees poured into the German ports on the Baltic Sea. They queued and fought to get on to ships as the Soviet soldiers drew closer. Then, when the war was over, many countries like Poland were freed from German control. Lots of them hated the Germans. They threw them out of their countries. In all sixteen million Germans and East Europeans trudged back towards Germany.

The United Nations

At the end of the war there were millions of refugees. The United Nations tried to help. It set up a group to help refugees. The group built camps and gave food and clothing. They helped people to make a new life. A great deal of the money for the camps and so on came from the USA. Most other countries had fought for so long that they had no money left.

A SOURCE

When I was in Berlin you could get any German to do anything for a bar of chocolate or a loaf of bread.

Told to Fiona Reynoldson in 1972, by a British soldier who had been in Berlin in 1945.

B SOURCE

By 1946 European food production was half its pre-war level.

From 'The Times Atlas of the Second World War', 1989.

C SOURCE

Hitler's Germany employed slave labour in the factories, mines and farms. Thus the Germans shifted many people all over Europe.

From B. Catchpole, 'Map History of the Modern World', 1982.

Questions

1 Read the first sentence. What is a refugee?

2 Read the paragraph **Europe at the end of the war**.
   a Who advanced into Germany at the end of the war?
   b How many refugees went back to Germany?

3 Design a poster asking for help for refugees. What would they need? (food, jobs....)

4 Read Source F.
   a How many people was the ship supposed to carry?
   b How many was it carrying when it sank?
   c Who were the refugees running away from?
   d Many more Germans died in this disaster than on the *Titanic*. Yet we know more about the *Titanic*. Choose the most likely reason for this from the list below.

   The story was made up.
   The Germans lost the war, so no one cared if they died.
   Lots of refugees were dying everywhere.
   No journalists reported it.

E

SOURCE

16 million refugees trudged towards the west. Two million died.

F

SOURCE

The Wilhelm Gustloff was a big ship. Normally it carried 1,900 people. On the night of 30 January 1945, 8,000 refugees crowded on board. A Russian submarine spotted the ship making its way through the choppy ice cold sea. The ship was torpedoed and sunk. Everyone died.

From Fiona Reynoldson, 'Evacuees', 1990.

5.4 The End of Empires

What is an empire?

An **empire** is when one country rules land in other countries. The countries that are ruled are called **colonies**. At the end of the war Britain, France, the Netherlands, Belgium and Portugal were all imperialist powers with colonies in Africa and Asia. Within twenty years they had lost these empires.

Why did the imperialist powers lose their empires?

First, many of the colonies in Africa and Asia wanted to be free to run their own countries. Furthermore they did not like the imperialist powers taking raw materials like rubber, tin, copper and so on from the colonies and so making lots of money.

Second, the Second World War lasted six years. All the fighting weakened Europe. Countries such as Britain had not got the money or enthusiasm to fight to keep their empires.

Asia

During the war the European colonies had been taken by the Japanese. This showed the colonies that the Europeans could be beaten. After the war they fought for freedom. The people of Indochina wanted freedom so they fought the French from 1948–1954. They succeeded and made the new countries of North Vietnam, South Vietnam, Laos and Cambodia. The Dutch tried to get Indonesia back but the Indonesians would not let them. The same things happened in Africa.

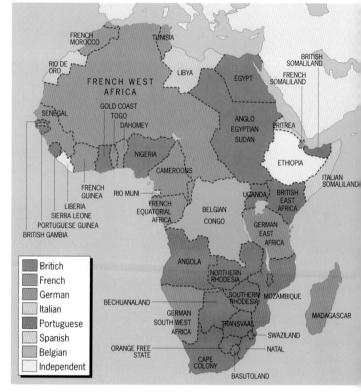

Africa in 1900.

British
French
German
Italian
Portuguese
Spanish
Belgian
Independent

A SOURCE

India was valued as a market for British goods and as a source of soldiers for the British army.

W. O. Simpson, 'Changing Horizons, 1986'.

B SOURCE

To have stayed in India for a moment longer would have broken Britain financially and militarily.

Lord Ismay, 'The Memoirs of Lord Ismay', 1960. India gained its independence from Britain in 1947.

India

India was part of the British Empire. It had long wanted to be free. Britain was exhausted by the war and granted independence in 1947. The two new independent countries were called India and Pakistan.

Africa

Many countries in Africa also began to win their independence. Countries like Britain came to accept that they would no longer control the freedom of the people of Africa (see Source D).

Today, the wind of change is blowing through Africa. We must all accept it as a fact.

SOURCE

Harold Macmillan, the British Prime Minister, speaking in 1960.

SOURCE

The Indonesians had been successful partly because of sympathy from other countries; partly because the Netherlands (Holland) was a small, far away country weakened by the Second World War and partly because enough Indonesians were prepared to fight.

'History of the Twentieth Century', 1968, explaining why the Netherlands failed to retake part of its empire in Asia.

Questions

1 What is (a) an empire and (b) a colony?

2 Read page 86 and Source D. What do you think Macmillan meant by 'the wind of change'? Choose from the list below.
   * the weather is getting worse in Africa
   * Britain will have to change the way it rules its colonies in Africa
   * The colonies in Africa want freedom to rule themselves.

SOURCE

A Dutch army poster. It is aimed at recruiting soldiers to keep the Dutch colony in Indonesia.

5.5 The Beginnings of the Cold War

The USSR

The USSR was a communist country. Farms, factories and so on were owned by all the workers and run by the government to make a profit for the workers. This sounded fine, but in reality, Stalin, the head of the government turned out to be a dictator. He kept control of everything himself. He did not allow anyone to criticize the government.

The USA and Western Europe

The USA and Western Europe were capitalist countries. Farms, factories and companies were owned by individual people who ran them to make a profit for themselves. These sort of people did not like the idea of communism at all. As far as running the country was concerned, however, the governments were elected by the people of the country. They could criticize the government if they wanted to. So these capitalist countries were also democratic.

After the Second World War

The USA and USSR had fought as allies to defeat Nazi Germany. But after the war the USA was afraid that the USSR was spreading communism to other countries. The USSR was afraid that the USA would set out to destroy communism and end up attacking the USSR.

The Cold War

The USA and the USSR did not go to war. But they distrusted each other and looked on each other as enemies. This was called the Cold War.

B

SOURCE

At the moment countries can either have free elections and democracy or be run by a government which allows people no freedom.

From a speech by President Truman, in 1947.

A

SOURCE

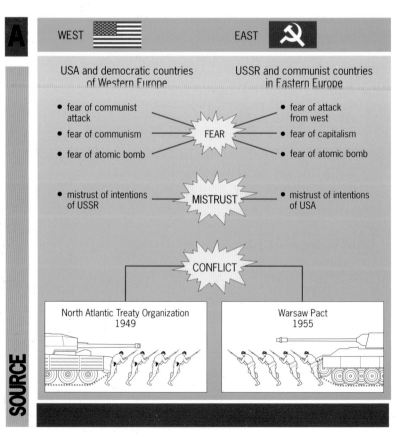

The Cold War: The product of fear.

The USA, the Truman Doctrine and the Marshall Plan

In 1947 President Truman said that the USA would help any country in the world which felt threatened by communism. This upset the USSR.

Shortly after this, the USA offered to give money to the countries of Western Europe to help them recover from the war. They could use the money to build new factories, ships and so on. This was called the **Marshall Plan**. The USA was keen to make sure Western Europe was strong and rich so that it would resist communism and the USSR.

NATO (1949) and the Warsaw Pact (1955)

NATO was the North Atlantic Treaty Organization. It was an alliance of ten Western European countries plus Canada and the USA. A few years later the USSR joined with Eastern European countries to form the Warsaw Pact. Both sides were armed to the teeth and ready to fight if necessary.

Question

1 Read page 88. Write out the sentences below. Choose the correct word from the brackets each time.
The USSR was a (competent/communist) country. Everything was owned by the (workers/walkers) and run by the government. The USA was a (capitalist/capable) country. Everything was owned and run by (lots of/individual) people. Everyone had a vote. This was called a (dreamland/democracy).

C

SOURCE

A Soviet poster accusing the Americans of developing chemical weapons. The three barrels are labelled 'The Plague, Cholera, and Typhus'. At the front of the vehicle the American Secretary of State is saying to the Secretary-General of the United Nations, 'The USA does not use chemical weapons.'

5.6 From Confrontation to Co-operation

The Cold War

The Cold War lasted for nearly fifty years. Sometimes the two sides got on better. Sometimes they got on a lot worse. There were five important incidents when they got on so badly that an outright war was possible.

1 The Berlin Airlift 1948

After the war the German city of Berlin was divided in two. The USSR held East Berlin and the USA and Western allies held West Berlin. In 1948, the relations between the USSR and USA were so bad that the USSR closed all the roads and railways into West Berlin. The USA was worried. It looked as though the USSR was going to take more and more land in Europe. So the USA and its allies held on to West Berlin by flying in food and goods day and night. After a year the USSR reopened the roads and railways.

2 Hungary

In 1956 Hungary was not allowed to leave the Warsaw Pact. The USSR invaded Hungary and crushed all opposition. The West was horrified.

A SOURCE

The steel-shod Soviet [USSR] jackboot heeled down on Hungary this week.

Comment on the USSR's invason of Hungary in the American magazine, 'Time'.

B SOURCE

It was 10.25 a.m. A messenger brought in a note, 'Mr President, the Soviet ships have stopped and turned round.'

Robert Kennedy, the President's brother, remembers the Cuban Missile crisis of 1962.

The threat to the USA from Soviet missiles on Cuba.

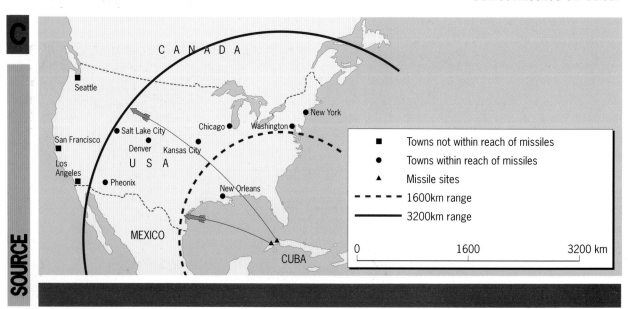

C SOURCE

Map showing Canada, USA, Mexico and Cuba with missile ranges.

Legend:
- ■ Towns not within reach of missiles
- ● Towns within reach of missiles
- ▲ Missile sites
- – – – 1600km range
- —— 3200km range

Scale: 0 — 1600 — 3200 km

3 West and East Berlin

In 1961 the USSR built a huge wall between East and West Berlin so that no one could cross from one side to the other. If they did try they were shot.

4 Cuba

In 1962 USA spy planes discovered that the USSR was building missile bases on the island of Cuba which meant USSR missiles could be launched against the USA. The USA sent warships to stop the missiles reaching Cuba. This meant USA and USSR ships might clash and start a war. The world held its breath. The USSR ships stopped. After this a direct teleprinter line was set up between the USA and USSR so they could negotiate a bit better.

5 Czechoslovakia

In 1968 Czechoslovakia rebelled against the USSR. As with Hungary the USSR crushed the rebellion. This upset people in the West.

1985 onwards

Mikhail Gorbachev became leader in the USSR. He set out to be more friendly with the West and to have better living conditions at home.

From 1989, many of the people in places like Czechoslovakia and Hungary demanded freedom from the USSR. Soon even the Berlin Wall was torn down and the Cold War between East and West was over. Then in 1991 the Communist Party was overthrown and the USSR was broken up.

Questions

1 Read **The Cold War**. How long did the Cold War last for?

2 Read **Cuba**.
   a What did the USA spy planes discover in 1962?
   b Why was the USA so worried about the missile bases in Cuba?

1989: The end of the Warsaw Pact	
5 June:	Communist Party defeated in Polish elections.
10 Sept:	Hungary opens border with Austria. Thousands flee.
1 Oct:	Czechoslovakia opens borders. Thousands flee.
9 Nov:	Berlin Wall is breached in East Germany.
10 Nov:	Bulgarian communist dictator, Zhikov, overthrown.
24 Nov:	Czech Communist Party leaders resign.
22 Dec:	Romanian dictator, Ceausescu, overthrown and executed.

Communism comes to an end.

A happy crowd help tear up the Berlin Wall in November 1989.

SOURCE

D

6.1 The Changing World

The world has changed a great deal in the last hundred years.

Transport

A hundred years ago there were few cars and no aeroplanes. Very few people made long journeys. For instance, it took at least five days to go by ship from Britain to the USA. Nowadays it takes only a few hours in an aeroplane.

A hundred years ago cars had only just been invented. Now there are about 400 million cars in the world.

Communications

Because of the advances in technology, particularly telephone lines and satellites it is possible to telephone or fax almost anywhere in the world. It is possible to watch television or listen to radio from anywhere in the world. Computers (via telephone lines) link businesses all over the world.

Medicine

Medical technology has advanced a great deal. Hearts, livers, kidneys and lungs can be replaced in long complicated operations. There are many powerful drugs to kill infections. Advances in electronics have enabled medical engineers to make new machines that can see inside the body so that they can find out what is wrong with

A SOURCE

Boeing 747s in flight.

B SOURCE

More and more people now own television sets and video recorders.

it. However, traditional medicine is still used in many countries by many people. This includes acupuncture, herbal medicine and faith healing.

Engineering

Engineers have always built things like roads, tunnels and buildings. They can now build them faster, bigger and better. They can also build smaller things which have changed peoples' lives even more. These include washing machines, microwave ovens and freezers. Many of these things have given more chance for people to have leisure time.

The Developing World

Meanwhile, in many parts of the developing world people still do not have enough to eat, let alone having cars and telephones. Even in the richer countries, unemployment means that there can be great differences in the way people live.

The environment

The environment is all around us, including the air we breathe and the land we grow our food on. Many people are worried that we are poisoning the land and the air, with chemicals and waste products. They are worried that we are killing off animals such as the fish in the sea, and plants such as trees.

More governments are trying to stop damage to the environment but in the end it is up to all of us. Stopping any further damage will almost certainly mean that people in the rich countries like the USA, France, Germany and Britain will have to have a lower standard of living. Washing powders can pollute rivers and lakes. Gases from cars and smoke from power stations (to heat our homes) cause smog and so on.

C SOURCE

Britain and the Undeveloped World in 1991				
Country	GDP per person (in US dollars)	Literacy Rate	Life Expectancy Male	Female
Britain	16,750	99%	73	79
Ethiopia	120	66%	43	49
Laos	230	84%	50	53
Bangladesh	220	35%	53	53
Haiti	370	53%	55	58
Yemen	540	39%	52	52

GDP stands for 'Gross Domestic Product'. This is the value of the goods and services produced in a year. The grid shows one way of comparing the standards of living between different countries.

D SOURCE

Possibly as many as two thirds of the world's children go to bed hungry every night. In a country where there is not enough food, parents have a real feeding problem: how to fill their children's stomachs. There is no question of children refusing to eat whatever is offered.

From Dr. Hugh Jolly, 'Book of Child Care', 1978.

Political changes – the break up of the USSR

In 1989 the Berlin Wall came down. Berlin became one city again. East and West Germany became one country again. The following years saw the breakup of the old USSR into separate countries. These countries, like Latvia and Estonia, are now represented in their own right in international sport.

Political changes – South Africa

In 1990 **apartheid** came to an end in South Africa. Black people, at last, were given equal voting rights with white people. In 1994 **Nelson Mandela** became the first black president of South Africa.

Air pollution in Los Angeles, California, USA (see page 93).

Political changes – Europe

Europe is slowly moving towards union. The member countries of the European Union are wondering whether to have a single currency and, eventually, one parliament in Brussels.

All these changes would have been unthinkable just a few years ago – and yet they have happened. Whatever the future holds, great effort and tolerance will be needed to meet the coming changes and to ensure the safety of the planet.

Questions

1 Read **Communications**. Write out the sentence below choosing the correct word from the brackets each time. (Tractors/telephone lines) and (electric lights/satellites) have made it possible to link places all over the world.

2 Look at Source C
   a How long can you expect to live as a female in Laos?
   b How long can you expect to live if you are a female in Britain?
   c Which country has the lowest GDP per person?
   d Is there any relationship between income and life expectancy?

3 Read Source D. Does Source D support Source C?

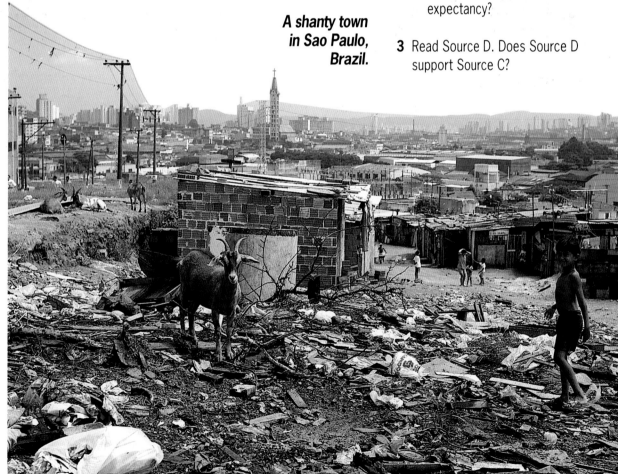

A shanty town in Sao Paulo, Brazil.